MARBLEHEAD
MYTHS, LEGENDS AND LORE

Marblehead

Myths, Legends and Lore

From Storied Past to Modern Mystery

To Liz,
You are always
welcome in
Marblehead!
Love,
Pamy

Pam Matthias Peterson

Pam M. Peterson

Charleston · London

THE
History
PRESS

Published by The History Press
Charleston, SC 29403
www.historypress.net

Cover Images (clockwise from top left):
This portrait depicts King Philip, the Native American sachem or chief who led the rebellion known as King Philip's War. *Illustration from* Nooks and Corners of New England, *S.A. Drake, 1875. Portrait of Elbridge Gerry*, after an engraving. *Illustration from* Nooks and Corners of New England, *S.A. Drake, 1875.* J.O.J. Frost, circa 1920s. The artist is holding his carved and painted cod. *Courtesy of the Marblehead Museum & Historical Society.* Marblehead Harbor, from the journals of Ashley Bowen. Dated 1763, this is believed to be the earliest view of the town. *Courtesy of the Marblehead Museum & Historical Society.*

First published 2007
Second printing 2008

Manufactured in the United States

ISBN 978.1.59629.256.7

Library of Congress Cataloging-in-Publication Data

Peterson, Pam Matthias.
  Marblehead myths, legend and lore / Pam Matthias Peterson.
      p. cm.
  Includes bibliographical references and index.
  ISBN 978-1-59629-256-7 (alk. paper)
  1. Tales--Massachusetts--Marblehead. 2. Marblehead (Mass.)--Folklore. I. Title.
  GR110.M4P48 2007
  398.209744'5--dc22
                                2007017132

Notice: The information in this book is true and complete to the best of our knowledge. It is offered without guarantee on the part of the author or The History Press. The author and The History Press disclaim all liability in connection with the use of this book.

Contents

Acknowledgements

I would never presume to call myself a Marbleheader. I've only lived here for about thirty years, and that doesn't count. I'm not a native, and have no connection with the town except what has been forged through living, working and loving everything connected with it. It has been a great place to raise a family, to make friends and establish a life. The history of Marblehead is a fascinating source of connections, significant both locally and in the wider world. Most of all, Marblehead itself is the inspiration for this book.

I feel very fortunate to have had the support of my family, my husband, my children Matthew and Joie and the great help of many friends. Paula Morse read the manuscript with her talented skill, care and perception. Anna Geraghty helped with photos and as always went above and beyond what was asked. My friends and colleagues at the Marblehead Museum & Historical Society, staff and volunteers, provided laughter, encouragement and constant interruptions as they always do. Many thanks to Karen MacInnis, Judy Anderson, Cinny Rockett, Joan Goloboy, Marcia Hunkins and everyone else. Thanks also to Gene Arnould, Judy Jacobi and Nick and Susan Fader.

Introduction
Marblehead Myths and Legends

Myths and legends can be important clues to cultural history. A place is shaped by its myths and they in turn shape it. Stories are told long before they are written down; many folk tales are added to, adapted or changed before the final version is reached. Myths and legends generally have within them a kernel of truth, and that is of interest to historians. Legends can represent a link or a lead to wonderful information or insight hidden within the story, a starting place in the hunt for historical treasure. Although many stories that we know and love would be discarded as they are not fact, they must not be ignored as primary sources of oral history.

Marblehead is a town that is unusually rich in myths and legends. Fishermen are well known as storytellers, and have a reputation for making their tales a bit larger than the truth, so perhaps that is an ingredient in some of the great Marblehead myths. Marblehead is also rich in history, and many of these stories are true. Some of them began with a few facts and were embroidered and adapted until they reached their present form. All of the tales help to shape a true picture of Marblehead. They date from the earliest times, when stories were handed down among friends and family for protection, enjoyment and pride in the good old town, and continue through the centuries to the present. The history of the town is interwoven with its culture, and all of these myths and legends come together to make the history of Marblehead's people, places and events.

Chapter 1.

Early Times and Early Stories

To start at the beginning, Marblehead was first a fishing station, serving as an outpost for fishermen. Gradually families began to arrive and Marblehead was established as a village in 1629. All activities were related to the fishing trade. The town grew up around Little Harbor, where the first meetinghouse was built on Old Burial Hill. From this vantage point the small settlement could look out to sea. Fishing schooners went out beyond the protection of the harbor, fishing mostly for cod.

The lives of fishermen and their families were uncertain. The fishing vessels were small, the seas were rough, the weather was unpredictable and the coastline was rocky. There were many dangers for fishermen, and their lives were hard. Fishing is a cold, wet, physically demanding job at the best of times. Fishermen and their families were superstitious, always looking for signs and omens. They were largely uneducated and very much at the mercy of external forces that they often did not understand and could not control.

Fish Tale

One of the earliest myths goes back to the time of settlement in the early 1600s, when Marblehead was a fishing outpost and English investors were anxious to encourage new settlers to come here. Many

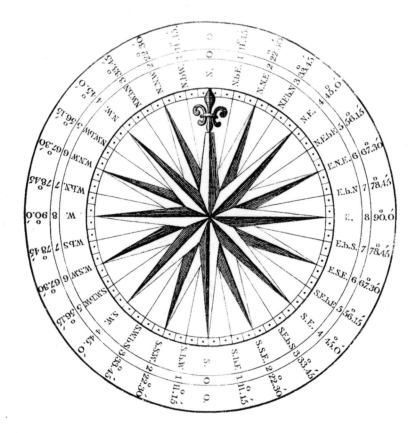

Mariners' Compass, engraving. *Illustration from* The Practical Navigator, *London, 1793.*

tales were told of the colonies in the New World to enhance their image and encourage immigrants. Captain John Smith wrote of the advantages of fishing as a trade, and King James piously added, "In truth 'tis an honest trade, 'twas the apostles' own calling."

There are several accounts of the huge quantity of fish in the harbor at Marblehead. These fish were reported to be so large and the harbor so full of them that a person could walk from one side of the harbor to the other on the backs of them without ever getting his feet wet. Fishermen continually rejoiced in the variety and abundance of their catch. This story is repeated over and over about Marblehead, and also about other colonial areas that were good fishing grounds. It could not possibly be true, but it is in a sense an advertising claim, like the streets being paved with gold, which was exaggerated to advertise Marblehead and to attract new colonists.

The First Settler

The first settler was named Doliber. There is a possible first name of John, but no actual dates are associated with this legendary person. He was said to have left Salem when the customs and laws of that Puritan town became too stifling and he floated across Salem Harbor in a giant hogshead barrel to Marblehead's opposite west shore. He used the barrel as his home and lived in it at what is still known as Doliber's Cove.

There are no records of this event, and nothing to substantiate it, although the Doliber family name appears in Marblehead's earliest records and certainly Dolibers were among the first settlers. There have always been and still remain members of the Doliber family who are prominent in Marblehead and dedicated to the continuation of the town's history.

Native Americans

When the first English settlers came to Marblehead there were very few Native Americans left in the area. Marblehead's great harbor and the west shore continually reveal signs of earlier Native American presence in arrowheads, fragments of tools, bits of shell and other signs that this area had been a fertile fishing ground and seasonal settlement for centuries.

All of the Native American tribes of the Northeast were nomadic. They followed the seasons to find food and moved from place to place. The Naumkeags, part of the Algonquin nation of woodland tribes, came to Marblehead for the same reason that people come today. In the summer it is beautiful; fishing and living by the shore is a relaxed and healthful way to spend the time. For the Naumkeags, Marblehead in the summer was part of their route. They used the time to fish, clam and collect shells; particularly prized were mussel shells with beautiful iridescent purple insides. They also collected salt from the ocean shores.

Nanapashemet was the sachem, or chief, in the time of early settlement. After his death in 1617, his wife became the Squaw Sachem and she ruled with the help of her three sons, called sagamores. Their Anglicized names were James, John and George. Relations between

This portrait depicts King Philip, the Native American sachem or chief who led the rebellion known as King Philip's War. *Illustration from* Nooks and Corners of New England, *S.A. Drake, 1875.*

the Naumkeags and the European settlers were generally peaceful, and there was little conflict between the two groups. This was the case in large part because the tribe had already been decimated by tribal wars and disease before the white settlers appeared. But from time to time there were conflicts. Certainly there was tension and fear on both sides, as many stories of gruesome deeds were known to settlers and Native Americans alike.

The Squaw Sachem and Sagamore George were owners of the land that included Marblehead. As the seventeenth century progressed, Native American presence became almost nonexistent in the town, with the exception of minor trade for goods. However, all of New England was horrified by the violence and brutality of King Philip's War in 1675, which was the last stand of the New England tribes against encroaching white settlers. Although there had appeared to be peace and harmony with tribes in the region, including many religious conversions that produced the "Praying Indians," as they were called, there was resentment, fear and anger under the surface. White settlers seemed to increase every day, and to expand their range farther and farther into Indian land. Finally, there was an all-out war by the frustrated and angry tribal leaders. Led by King Philip, sachem of several tribes, there was a bloody war, mostly in the area of central Massachusetts. Sagamore George took part in the war. As a result, he, along with many other Native Americans who survived, was sold into slavery in the West Indies. They were bought to work on the sugar plantations, mainly in Jamaica.

The use of Native American slaves was in fact the initial plan of plantation owners in the American South as well as in the Caribbean islands. They knew they needed cheap labor to work their large fields, and had thought the native population would be the answer. In general the Native Americans proved disappointing, since they did not do well in captivity and tended to die. It was then that the traffic in slaves from Africa began.

The Ship *Desire*

In 1636 the ship *Desire* was built in Marblehead. It was the third large vessel built in the American colonies, and the early settlers were very proud of her. The *Desire*'s captain was William Pierce, considered one of the finest mariners and navigators of his day. He was renowned for his naval skill, having set a record for crossing the Atlantic in twenty-three days. Pierce spent most of his career traveling back and forth across the Atlantic Ocean, carrying passengers and cargo from England to the American colonies. Even before King Philip's War, he was one of many who transported defeated Native American warriors to the West Indies to serve as slaves on sugar plantations. On a return voyage he brought a cargo that included black slaves to the New England colonies. This was the first recorded slave transaction.

It is interesting that stories of the *Desire*, and in fact knowledge of the ship in general, have almost disappeared. What was once a source of pride, as an early sign of colonial ingenuity and skill, has now become a source of shame. No one wants to remember the *Desire* any longer, as it cannot be separated from its cargo of human suffering. Now that social conscience is aware of all the interconnections of slavery, and aware that there was guilt in the North as well as the South, it is a topic that makes everyone uncomfortable. Myths and legends can be and are edited all the time.

Marblehead Women's Revenge

Another after effect of King Philip's War relates to Marblehead. There was horrible cruelty in this war and many colonials, including innocent women and children, were tortured and killed by bands of Native Americans who went to settlements and outposts looking for them. Accounts of brutal death and mutilation of women and children were common. These stories were told by soldiers and travelers, and the tales made their way to Marblehead.

After the war was over, some of the defeated Native Americans were being taken through the town to a ship to be transported to the West Indies. As they passed by, they were attacked and captured by the incensed women of Marblehead. Then they were tarred, feathered and dragged through the streets. Fear and disgust at the stories of horrible violence to women and young children had incensed them and caused the Marblehead women to take action against the enemy.

This tale was told as a tribute to their independent strength and spirit; fishermen's wives were left alone for months at a time to fend for themselves and their families with no support other than their own resources. These women managed in all circumstances, but this story survives because it describes their vicious and unwavering defense of their homes and families. It is a genuine "don't mess with me" story that may have given villains pause when they thought about attacking other defenseless women.

Marblehead for Sale

After King Philip's War, English magistrates and officials began to consider the legality of the possession of lands that had been taken in the name of the Crown. They decided that they needed signed deeds to prove ownership, and that Native American tribes should be compensated for their lands—not too much, but enough to make it legal. All towns and villages were ordered to procure a legal document from the original owners of their land.

In Marblehead this posed a small problem. Technically Sagamore George was the principal owner, along with his mother and his wife. However, he was in slavery in Jamaica. The Squaw Sachem refused to sign the deed until her son was returned. So the hunt was on for Sagamore George. He was found, put on a ship and returned to Marblehead. He was reunited with his family, but Sagamore George died before the document was signed.

The parchment deed, which still hangs in Marblehead's Abbot Hall, shows the mark of his mother as well as that of his wife. The town was sold for eighty pounds, and all was legal and in order. There is also a painting at Abbot Hall of the signing of the deed of sale. It is by Marblehead folk artist J.O.J. Frost. The scene looks idyllic, with Native Americans and English settlers smiling and happy. Just like stories of Plymouth and other early settlements, these myths of friendly and peaceful relations with the Native Americans, with the Indians cheerfully handing over their land and their rights in gleeful exchange for a bit of money and a handful of beads, were created as propaganda after the fact.

In the late nineteenth and early twentieth centuries the "Noble Savage" became a popular hero, and people told the stories they wanted to hear about the early settlement of America. They didn't change the basic facts; they just left out the nasty bits. This meant that everyone could look back on these days of early settlement with a clear conscience. It was made easier because there were no written records from the Native Americans, and virtually no survivors to tell the tale.

The Fisherman's Return

When Marblehead fishing schooners went to the Grand Banks to fish for cod and halibut, they were often gone for several months. While away the fishing vessels received no mail or any communication, except occasional news from another schooner recently arrived on the Banks, and even that was rare.

Once there was a young fisherman who had been fishing for a long stretch of time. He and all the crew were eager to get back home, and they were glad when the fishing vessel's hold was finally full of fish and the return journey was begun. When the little fishing schooner sailed into Marblehead Harbor, everyone was happy to be home. The young fisherman was especially pleased because then he could go to see his sweetheart, the girl he was betrothed to wed. When the ship was anchored and the young fisherman could get away he went quickly to his loved one's house. He brought some fresh fish from the catch as a special gift. She opened the door and greeted him with great joy. They kissed and spent the evening together, planning for their future.

Then the fisherman went home and let himself into his parents' house, planning to have his homecoming with them in the morning. The next morning when he saw his mother and father, they seemed sad. His mother embraced him and started to cry. The young man asked what was wrong. They said, "We are so sorry to tell you that your sweetheart died while you were away."

"What?" he cried. "It can't be true. I saw her last night and brought her fish from the catch." The young man and his parents ran to his sweetheart's cottage. It stood quiet, closed and dusty inside. But on the kitchen table were the fish, the last gift of the young fisherman to his true love.

Tom Bowen's Church

The meetinghouse that stood on Old Burial Hill was built around 1638. Worshippers went there to hear Marblehead's unordained minister, William Walton, to meet their friends and neighbors, to visit and to gossip. They went summer and winter, and in winter they brought along their dogs to keep their feet warm, as dogs were allowed to sleep under the pews.

Many people went to the meetinghouse, but some townspeople still preferred to go to Salem to attend the Puritan church. To do so they traveled by ferry. They went over to the West Shore, where Tom Dixey ran a ferry service to take passengers across Salem Harbor. Just beside the ferry dock was a tavern owned by Tom Bowen. Some of the husbands didn't quite make it to all the way down the dock to the ferry, choosing instead to attend "Tom Bowen's Church." This

Old Burial Hill, photograph. *Courtesy of the Marblehead Museum & Historical Society.*

story is still quite popular in Marblehead, as there seem to be quite a few people who wish that Tom Bowen's establishment was still an option.

Marblehead prospered as a fishing village and by 1660 the king's agents declared Marblehead to be "the greatest Towne for fishing in New England." The small settlement grew and Marbleheaders became known as hardworking, hard-living individuals. Marblehead was a part of Salem until 1649, when it broke away to become a separate incorporated town. It had been distinctly different from Salem from the beginning, as Salem was settled by religious pilgrims, Puritans who came to the new world with a desire to create a place where they could worship as they chose and establish a community of faith and order. Marblehead was settled by fishermen who came to the new world to fish. They were not particularly concerned or interested in any form of government or religion. The early court records are full of accounts of Marblehead men and women being brought into court for offenses such as not attending church or observing the Sabbath, public drunkenness, use of foul language and other behavior that was condemned by Salem town officials. The separation of Marblehead and Salem into two different towns was undoubtedly a relief to all concerned.

Chapter 2.

Magic, Witches and Fortune Telling

Physical surroundings and conditions in earlier times help to explain why myths and legends became so important and why people told the stories as cautionary tales, or to give each other hope and courage. These stories were believed because they offered at least some explanation or possible solution to often inexplicable events. The night and its darkness were fearful and full of danger and people did not go out after dark if they could help it for very good reasons. When they did, they lighted their way with lantern, torch or moonlight, and the night was full of shadows and sounds. Dim lighting and strange sounds all contributed to mysterious events that could not be explained except by fantastic stories. The stories also served as a warning to the foolhardy to think twice about going out and about in the dark, to protect them from danger. The legends also offered hope that sometimes things turned out better than anyone could imagine. People wanted to believe that there were forces beyond human understanding that sometimes could help.

Wizard Dimond

In Marblehead there lived a retired ship's captain named Edward Dimond. He was referred to as Wizard Dimond, and many people believed, as he did himself, that he had special powers. The Wizard wore a large cape and was a strong, imposing and respected old man. On stormy nights Wizard Dimond could be found up at the top of Burial Hill, cape swirling in the wind, railing at the forces of nature and calling out to the fishing schooners at sea. He called to the fishing vessels and their crews by name and shouted commands to the forces of nature. He demanded that the winds and rough seas become calm and send the ships safely home to Marblehead Harbor. When local wives and families were worried, they paid a visit to Wizard Dimond's house. They begged him to intercede for loved ones and their vessels. There were many tales from sailors and fishermen claiming that when onboard ship they clearly heard Wizard Dimond's voice above the wind and waves calling them home. He lived at the foot of Old Burial Hill in a house called the Old Brig. It still stands today, and was supposedly built from parts of a ship.

Townspeople also came to Wizard Dimond when they had troubles on land. They respected his fairness and sense of justice. At one time a poor widow of Marblehead was the victim of theft. All her wood for the winter had been stolen and she came to Wizard Dimond for help. She was distraught, as she could not afford to buy more, and was afraid she would freeze to death in the coming winter. Old Dimond discovered the thief, chastised him for his evil deed and made him replace all the wood. Then it was said that the Wizard exacted a magical punishment. He put a spell on the man so that he had to walk all night with a heavy log attached to his back that he couldn't remove. He was forced to walk back and forth from his house to the widow's cottage from sunset to sunrise without stopping. By morning he was dropping with fatigue, and surely must have learned his lesson. The Wizard's spell had also seen to it that others who might have had the idea to steal wood from defenseless widows would think twice about it.

Moll Pitcher

Wizard Dimond had a granddaughter named Moll, who also had special powers. She could see into the future, cure some ailments with herbs and she was good at making love potions and charms. When she married and moved to Lynn, she became Moll Pitcher (no relation or connection to Moll or Molly Pitcher of Revolutionary War fame) and was a well-known fortune teller. People traveled from all over the North Shore and beyond to seek her advice.

Moll Pitcher was born in 1738 in her grandfather's house, the Old Brig, on Orne Street in Marblehead. Her father, Aholiab Dimond, was a cordwainer or shoemaker, and he took an apprentice named Robert Pitcher. Moll and Richard fell in love and were married. They moved to Lynn and lived at the foot of High Rock. Their cottage soon became famous, as many visitors made their way there to consult Moll Pitcher and have their fortunes told. A neighbor across the street had a gate made of whale bones that came to be a landmark for those looking for Moll Pitcher's home, and an excuse for those embarrassed by their quest. Reluctant visitors sometimes claimed to have found her only because they were looking for the whale bone fence.

Many came looking, as Moll had inherited her grandfather's psychic powers. She had the ability to see into the future, and her skill as a prophetess was greatly sought after. It was written that "Royalty of Europe as well as simple maids of America sought to learn the future from her." Moll is said to have predicted the outcome of the Battle of Bunker Hill. General John Glover of Marblehead took Moll Pitcher to Cambridge to see General George Washington, where she raised his spirits greatly when she foretold his victory in the Revolutionary War. British generals, including Burgoyne, Pitcairn and Gage, also consulted the oracle. She is said to have gained more information from them than they did from her, and to have told it to Elbridge Gerry of Marblehead to help the patriotic cause.

Moll's husband either died young or was unable to work. In either case, she was left with four children to raise on her own. She used her fortune-telling abilities as a means of supporting her family. She was very successful and had clients from all walks of life. Sailors and sea captains refused to leave port if Moll predicted a bad voyage. Businessmen admitted her influence when they had to make investment decisions. Treasure hunters also consulted Moll, but she scoffed at them, saying, "Fools; if I knew where the money was buried do you think I would tell you?"

Like her grandfather Wizard Dimond, Moll was a protector of those less fortunate. She was known to regularly walk two miles before sunrise to take flour to a poor widow who would otherwise have no food for her children.

Moll Pitcher used cards and read palms, but her favorite way of telling fortunes was with tea leaves. She boiled the leaves and dumped them unstrained into her client's cup. The position of the tea leaves in the bottom of the cup decided the fate of the person seeking their fortune. It has been said, though, that all these methods were just a

Book cover from *The Celebrated Moll Pitcher's Prophecies*, Mrs. Ellen Griffen, Boston, 1895.

means to gain enough time for Moll to assess her clients and pick up vibrations from them.

All of Moll's interviews were conducted over a Queen Anne–style table that was small and round. It dates from about 1750 and is in the collection of the Marblehead Museum & Historical Society.

People from all over the world came to have their fortunes told by Moll Pitcher. But it was local people who sought her services most. Moll was consulted on affairs of love, loss of property and future fortunes. She was able to maintain a steady stream of customers because she had good perception and shrewd judgment. She also had an astonishingly good record of successful predictions.

Long after Moll's death there came to be a great deal of interest in what she had looked like. This stems in part from a poem by John Greenleaf Whittier entitled "Moll Pitcher," published in 1838. In the poem Whittier describes Moll as a "wasted, gray and meager hag." He goes on:

> She had the crooked nose of a witch,
> and in her gait she had a hitch,
> and in her hand she carried a switch
> to aid her in her work of sin.
> A twig of wizard hazel, which
> had grown beside a haunted ditch.

All in all, Whittier presented the perfect description of an evil witch. Though his poem was not very successful, this idea took hold for a time, and led to two "photographs" of Moll. One photo shows a wizened old woman, and is usually described as what Moll probably looked like. Since Moll Pitcher died in 1813, many years before photography was invented, this at least makes some sense. But a 1909 newspaper article announced with great excitement that the "genuine" photograph of Moll Pitcher had just been discovered. As Moll herself knew well, some people will believe anything.

This depiction of Moll Pitcher as a witch, however, was very upsetting to many people in Lynn, and in the late nineteenth century Moll Pitcher's grave received a stone marker that includes an engraved description of her appearance. "Moll Picher was of medium height and size for a woman, with good form and agreeable manners…Her countenance was intellectual, and she had the contour of face and expression which, without being positively beautiful, is nevertheless decidedly interesting…an eye when she looked at you of calm and keen penetration, and an expression of intelligent discernment half mingled with a glance of shrewdness." This was an attempt to recover Moll Pitcher's reputation as a good woman. Even though what Wizard Dimond and his daughter did sounds a lot like sorcery, they were never suspected of being witches, and were never accused or mistrusted.

The Witch of Marblehead: Mammy Redd

The end of the seventeenth century was a time of unrest in the American colonies. Many factors were at work, including the reassertion of English control over colonial government, concerns and threats about the French and Indians and a shift of influence and power away from the Puritan Church. In Boston, Cotton Mather was doing daily battle with his own nemesis, the Devil, whom he believed was at work everywhere. He saw the Devil's hand in all the problems that plagued the colonies. A recent outbreak of smallpox, the disfavor of the king of England and general uncertainty about the future were all attributed to the Devil. Mather published his account of Goody Glover, the witch of Boston, and described in detail how she took possession of children for evil purposes. Mather genuinely believed in the Devil and feared him. His work was definitely read by the Reverend Samuel Parris of Salem, and that it had an effect is evidenced by what happened in Salem.

Accusations of witchcraft and possession began in Salem Village in 1692. On May 28 the local constable came to arrest Wilmot Redd of Marblehead for having "committed sundry acts of witchcraft on the bodies of Mary Wolcott and Mercy Lewis and others in Salem Village to their great hurt." Wilmot, known as Mammy Redd, lived down by Redd's Pond. She was the wife of a poor fisherman, and she was old and disagreeable. She went out to do daily work around town, but she was not popular and never lasted very long in any one job. Wilmot Redd was accused by the "possessed" girls in Salem during the witch trials. None of them had ever seen her, though they claimed she flew on her broomstick from Marblehead to torment them. She was arrested, her hands bound and she was taken, standing in a horse-drawn cart, to Salem Village for questioning. When she appeared before the judges, in the presence of her accusers, several of the girls became hysterical at the sight of her. Mammy Redd was instructed to touch the girls, which apparently cured them of their hysterics. They testified that she had tormented them. Her response to all this was confusion and disbelief. When magistrates asked what she thought of the girls, she replied, "My opinion is they are in a sad condition." She was then indicted and charged with "detestable arts called witchcraft."

Mammy Redd was taken to Salem jail, and four months later her trial was held. Many witnesses from Marblehead were called but only a few appeared. They testified to earlier conflicts, and a curse that Mammy Redd had successfully cast on a previous employer. The curse she was accused of having cast was rather disgusting but effective. Her victim claimed she was unable to defecate for a month, which caused her stomach to swell and inflicted great pain. Then the depositions of the afflicted girls were read. They claimed that Mammy Redd flew to Salem to torment them, pinching them while they slept. Wilmot Redd refused to confess to being a witch, but there was no defense. No one from Marblehead came forward at the trial to speak on her behalf. She was convicted and hanged on September 22, 1692. No one, including her husband, ever helped her or brought her food or blankets at the jail. After her death her body was not claimed.

The witch hysteria in New England was short-lived overall. Salem was the center of the furor, but it had ramifications in other parts of New England. It finally ended when hysteria overcame common sense and the wife of Governor William Phipps was accused. Phipps reacted swiftly in defense of his wife and suddenly the frenzy was slowed. It was as if a bubble had burst. As awareness of the horror of what had been done began to sink in, there were public apologies and attempts to make amends. But nothing could bring back those who had already died, or make things better for the families who had lost their loved ones, their reputations or their property.

In fact, Wilmot Redd of Marblehead was one of many literally defenseless people who were persecuted at that time and are now remembered by a monument in Salem to the women and men who lost their lives during the witch trials.

Redd's Pond in Marblehead is named after Wilmot Redd, but she received far more recognition and concern in the twentieth century than she ever did in her own time. Mammy Redd is remembered as the only Marbleheader accused, tried and convicted in the Salem witch trials of 1692.

Black Joe, Aunt Creesy and Love Potions

In the eighteenth century there were many black freemen, sometimes freed slaves or sailors from faraway ports who came to live in New

England. Black Joe was a free man who lived in Marblehead and kept a tavern beside a small pond, known then and now as Black Joe's Pond. His real name was Joseph Brown, and he was able to read and write, or at least sign his name. Black Joe kept a good tavern and was well liked. He supplied food, drink and sometimes musical entertainment, and had a prosperous business.

Joseph Brown lived in Marblehead before, during and after the American Revolution. He became a member of Glover's Regiment and fought for independence. He is the only black man known to have been a part of the regiment, though it is probable that there were others. After the war, Black Joe came back to Marblehead, where he continued his business. His tavern was the scene of much merriment on Election Day, or "Lection Day" as it was known, a holiday that generated great excitement and celebration.

Though the actual location of Joseph Brown's grave is unknown, there is a gravestone marker for him on Old Burial Hill. It was placed there in 1976, for the bicentennial of the United States, to honor Black Joe and commemorate his service in the Revolutionary War.

Joseph Brown had a wife named Lucretia Brown, known to one and all as Aunt Creesy. Aunt Creesy cooked, kept the tavern tidy and was the originator of the famous Marblehead cookies known as Joe Froggers. They were large molasses cookies made in an iron skillet. When the batter hit the pan it ran in all directions, and formed shapes that looked like a frog's body and legs. Black Joe's Pond was the home of many frogs, and the association between the frogs and the cookies was made. Children often went to Black Joe's Pond to catch frogs and stopped at the tavern for cookies. As they got older, some of them, particularly the girls, went to Aunt Creesy for other things as well. They went to have their fortunes told and to get love potions. Although it wasn't exactly a secret, this service was usually sought after the sun went down. Groups of giggling girls, and sometimes intense, quiet ones, went to the kitchen door of the tavern to ask about their futures or to seek help to make their heart's desire come true.

A glimpse into the future is appealing at any age, but for young women of this time, the man they married was the determining factor in the success of their lives. Girls married young, and they knew the decision was important. Besides Aunt Creesy's fortune telling, there were many games and rituals that also gave girls a hint of their fate. One of these was a game that girls played with a ball

Tavern at Black Joe's Pond, built 1691. *Photograph by Judy Anderson, 2006.*

of yarn. They would gather in a friend's bedroom in the evening to visit, laugh and talk. Finally they would take up a ball of yarn. One girl had to lean halfway out the window and toss the yarn into the street. The young man who picked up the yarn would become that young lady's sweetheart. There must have been some sort of signal for eligible bachelors to know when this game was being played so that they could be waiting below. Another popular game for determining future husbands had to be played on the first night of the new moon. Girls gathered around a cauldron of boiling tallow and dropped hobnails, the kind of nails used for making boots, into the cauldron one by one. The young man who appeared when a girl was dropping her nail into the cauldron was destined to be her husband. The hobnails and boiling wax story has never made much sense, though it is repeated in all written accounts of Marblehead history and legend. It is an example of a story that has lost something in whisper-down-the-lane accounts told before it was written down. Perhaps even a part of the story itself is missing. When this happens, listeners realize that it is not a good story, and it will eventually fade away.

Marblehead's Cinderella

In the early eighteenth century there came to Marblehead a wealthy young Englishman of noble birth. His name was Sir Harry Frankland. He was heir to a title and lands in England. Because of his careless and scandalous behavior in England, his family arranged for him to be appointed colonial tax collector for the ports of Boston. He was sent to the colonies to give him some time to mature, and as a way to keep him from completely ruining his reputation in England. One of the ports under his jurisdiction was Marblehead, and it was on a visit there, when he stayed at the Fountain Inn on Marblehead's Little Harbor, that he saw a young and beautiful fisherman's daughter named Agnes Surriage.

Tradition has it that Agnes was scrubbing the steps of the inn when Sir Harry arrived, and he was immediately smitten. He is said to have been overwhelmed by her beauty, and appalled at her ragged clothing and bare feet. He gave her a gold coin to buy some shoes, and when he visited again a few weeks later he looked for her to see if she had purchased the shoes. She had, but she only wore them for special occasions, and not for her work at the Fountain Inn, and so he found her barefoot again. Sir Harry was quite taken with the young girl and negotiated with her father, a poor man, to allow Agnes to become his ward.

Sir Harry established her in a house in Boston, with a chaperone who taught her how to behave and dress and speak in polite society. Agnes and Harry fell in love. They eventually lived together as man and wife, but did not marry, as Sir Harry considered Agnes his social inferior. They lived in the North End of Boston, where they were shunned by polite society.

Then Sir Harry built a beautiful estate in Hopkinton, Massachusetts, where they invited those willing to visit. At Hopkinton there also lived a young man who was rumored to be their son. Upon Sir Harry's death many years later this young man inherited a fortune, seemingly confirming his parentage.

In the 1750s Sir Harry and Agnes went on a grand tour of the capitals of Europe, which included a visit to Lisbon, Portugal. They were there during the major earthquake in 1755. Sir Harry had just left their residence when the quake erupted and the road he was traveling on was split in two. His carriage capsized and was partially buried in rubble. Everyone was very frightened and there was confusion everywhere, but when Agnes learned of Harry's fate she ran down the road to find the carriage beneath a pile of stone. Largely through her own efforts and her strength of both mind and body, Agnes rescued him. In some versions of the story she hauled away huge rocks with her bare hands, and in other versions she began the job and commanded passersby to finish. It is often noted that she was typical of the women of Marblehead in that she was strong and determined, and therefore able to do this task. In any event, Sir Harry was saved and so overcome with gratitude that he finally asked Agnes to become his wife.

They returned to England, where Agnes, by then Lady Frankland, was greatly admired for her gracious and kind nature. She lived with Sir Harry until his death, and then married again. Agnes Surriage Frankland died in England in 1783. She is known as the Marblehead Cinderella.

Chapter 3.

Pirates

In the late seventeenth and early eighteenth centuries, pirates roamed the East Coast from the Caribbean to New England. Merchant ships that went between England and the colonies in New England, Virginia and the Caribbean islands carried treasures of goods and gold. They were irresistible to pirates, who captured the ships and smuggled, looted and plundered their cargo. New England seacoast villages were sometimes glad to see pirate ships and engage in a little smuggling themselves. They could acquire goods without paying any taxes, and in some cases a visit from a pirate ship wasn't at all bad. But pirates were unpredictable, and pirate ships regularly flew flags of peaceful nations to deceive their prey, switching to the Jolly Roger at the last minute when it was too late for their victims to get away.

Another trick of pirate vessels, when in need of water and supplies, was to watch for a fishing fleet to leave its small village and then sweep in to plunder. Pirates knew that when the fleet left, the village was virtually defenseless. All able-bodied men were at sea and only women, children and old men were left behind. Marblehead was in that state the night that pirates came ashore for a terrible deed that still sends shivers down the spines of many.

The Screaming Woman

Long ago, a Spanish ship was captured by pirates somewhere outside of Marblehead Harbor. The ship was full of treasure, with trunks of gold and jewels. Pirates knew that Marblehead's fishing fleet had left for the Grand Banks earlier that day. So they waited for nightfall to bring their prize into the shelter of Marblehead Harbor so that they could plunder her without being disturbed. Everyone on board the ship had been killed, and everyone on shore was too frightened to object.

It was a dark night, the moon shrouded in mist. The only survivor of the Spanish ship was a beautiful English lady passenger. She was dressed in an elegant gown of silk and wore many rings, necklaces and jewels. She had proudly refused to give up her possessions, and defied the pirates as best she could. Finally the pirates took her ashore to Lovis Cove in Marblehead Harbor. There they brutally murdered the poor woman, even chopping off her fingers to get the rings. The fine English lady screamed and begged for help from anyone who could hear her, "Lord save me! Mercy! O Lord Jesus, save me!" Her cries rang out over the lowland marshes that surrounded the cove. Many could hear, but they were defenseless against the pirates and so they stayed quiet to save themselves. Her screams went on and on until finally there was silence. The horror of the event was made worse because no one could or would save her. Perhaps it is for that reason that the place is still known as Screaming Woman's Cove, and her cries are still heard today. Even now people don't like to walk there late on dark and foggy nights, and every year there are reports of yet another person who has heard Marblehead's Screaming Woman.

Dungeon Rock

There is one story about pirates and their treasure that spans three centuries. It is a story that proves the power of myths and the desire to believe in them.

In the 1650s a pirate ship sailed up the Saugus River looking for a place to hide. The vessel was being hunted, and very likely had prisoners and stolen treasure on board. Finally they dropped anchor and four men left the ship and rowed ashore. They landed near the Saugus Iron Works, a seventeenth-century iron manufacturing site that still exists as a part of the National Park Service properties. Early the next morning workers at the ironworks found a letter requesting that shackles, handcuffs and hatchets be made. If these would be left in a secret place in the woods as soon as possible, payment would be made in silver coins. The men set to work at once and the order was quickly filled and left in the woods according to the instructions. The men received payment as promised. No one saw the pirate ship leave, but it was gone the same day.

Several months later the four men from the pirate ship were seen again, hiding in an area still known as Pirates Glen. Somewhat secluded, the area was ideally suited as a hiding place. According to the legend the pirates buried some of their treasure around Pirates Glen, and many treasure hunters have dug holes looking for it.

Townspeople were not the only ones to have seen the four men, and the king's ships soon appeared on the scene looking for the pirates. They tracked them to Pirates Glen and captured three of the four. The fourth pirate, named Thomas Veal, escaped through the woods. He went about two miles north to a cave in the Lynn Woods called Dungeon Rock. It was said that the pirates had already buried some of their treasure there. It was even rumored that Captain Kidd had buried some of his vast treasure in the area. Thomas Veal hid out and lived in the cave for several years, making his trade as a shoemaker. He was known to the people of Lynn, and the stories of his treasure were repeated often. Veal wore a sword and cutlass, and no one ever tried to steal his silver and gold. Why he had to make a living as a shoemaker if he had a great hidden treasure was never explained. Veal lived peacefully in the cave. By some accounts Veal was accompanied by a beautiful and exotic lady who wore many jewels, and by other accounts he lived alone.

In 1658 there was a terrible earthquake. It is well documented that an earthquake took place just north of Boston in that year. Thomas Veal was in his cave at Dungeon Rock at the time of the quake. He and his treasure were buried under a mountain of stone when the cave walls collapsed. The name Dungeon Rock refers to the fact that the cave became the pirate's dungeon or prison forever.

This story was told for almost two hundred years before it appeared in print in 1837 in *The Pirates Own Book*, an account of pirate stories from many sources and locations. The story also appeared in the first printed history of Lynn at about the same time. The power of the printed word is an amazing thing, and no one could ever have imagined the extraordinary result of the printing of this story. Shortly after the publication of these books, which described Dungeon Rock's location quite specifically, serious attacks on the cave began. A group of men exploded a keg of gunpowder at the mouth of the cave, hoping to expose Tom Veal's treasure. They only succeeded in burying what remained of the open cave in rock and rubble. There were several more somewhat random attempts on the cave, until finally came the most notable, prolonged and bizarre effort.

In the 1840s spiritualism became extremely popular both in the United States and England. Spiritualism is the belief and practice of communicating with the dead. Hiram Marble was an ardent spiritualist and he came to Dungeon Rock for the express purpose of finding Thomas Veal's treasure. He planned to accomplish this task by communicating with the dead pirate through mediums and clairvoyants. In 1852 Hiram Marble purchased five acres of land that included Dungeon Rock and began his project. He and his son Edwin built a house near the cave and cleared land for roads. That was the easy part. Then they moved on to the cave itself. There they began blasting and digging through solid rock. Every bit of stone removed from the cave was accomplished by following the directions of spirit guides. The spirits communicated through mediums. One of the spirit guides was said to be Yawata, daughter of the famous and powerful Native American Sachem Nanapashemet. At each séance, the mediums were given questions written by Hiram Marble on elaborately folded pieces of paper that remained unopened. This was supposed to be a way to prove that the communication with the spirits was not being tampered with.

From 1852 until 1880 this incredible project went on, with spirits leading the Marbles first this way, then that way through the rock. They never lost faith and when they were somewhat discouraged and feeling low, the spirit of the pirate sent a message:

> *Don't be discouraged. We are going as fast as we can. As to the course, you are in the right direction at present. You have only one more curve to make, before you take the curve that leads to the cave. We have a reason for keeping you from entering the cave at once. Moses was by the Lord kept 40 years in his circuitous route…ere he had sight of that land which flowed with milk and honey…Cheer up, Marble, we are with you and doing all we can.*
> *Your guide, Tom Veal*

Hiram Marble died in 1868, still believing that the treasure was there and that the spirits would lead him to it. His son Edwin continued the search until his death in 1880. He is buried at Dungeon Rock. His sister, Caroline Frances, continued to live at the site and give tours of the cave and show visitors the sword and scabbard of Tom Veal that her father and brother claimed to have found in the cave.

The Marble family was not successful in finding the treasure, and they did not achieve their goal of absolute proof that communication with the spirit world exists. But they did indirectly accomplish one part of their plan. They loved all the woods around Dungeon Rock and planned to use part of the treasure to purchase it and make the area into a public park. Shortly after Edwin Marble died, the city of Lynn purchased the land and named it Lynn Woods.

Dungeon Rock still exists, and there are still tours that take visitors down into the rock through narrow passages that twist and turn in a crazy pattern. And the treasure may still be there as well. Moll Pitcher's prophecy says, "The day will come when the rockbound secrets of Dungeon Cave will be revealed and the world will be astonished at the priceless gems discovered."

Marblehead Tunnels

The openings in the cave at Dungeon Rock are real enough. But in Marblehead there is an ongoing myth that is recounted frequently about the Marblehead tunnels. Many stories having to do with pirates, smuggling and secretive movements in general mention the labyrinth of tunnels under the town. At the King Hooper Mansion on Hooper Street there is a trap door that opens into the cellar of the house. The end of the cellar is supposedly blocked off, as it is an escape route to underground tunnels leading to the harbor. It is said that King Hooper used the tunnel for smuggling.

Out at the mouth of Marblehead Harbor, at Fort Sewall, there are caves in the rocks just below the fort. These caves are also said to lead to tunnels, again used for smuggling. The tunnels are supposed to run all over what is now known as the historic district, from one end of the old town to the other. This story is told by people who live in these houses and who go into their own basements and see that there is so much rock under their houses that the typical "Marblehead cellar" allows barely enough room for a person to stand. None of these cellars leads to tunnels.

All of Marblehead's downtown area is built on ledge rock. The only way there could possibly be tunnels under the town is if the early settlers in the seventeenth and early eighteenth centuries had access to explosives and for some reason spent large amounts of their time blasting holes in the rock, neither of which happened. Smuggling at that time was made relatively simple by the dark of night and several small islands for ships to hide behind. The caves at Fort Sewall were undoubtedly a hiding place for weapons, rum, fugitives and other items to be moved quietly without official interference. The caves are susceptible to the tide, and have now been permanently blocked up to prevent people from hiding in them and being drowned or washed out to sea at high tide. But the caves didn't lead anywhere. And yet the myth persists. Some stories are just too good to give up, even when they defy logic.

Marblehead's Robinson Crusoe

Accounts of pirates and their terrible deeds were well known by all sailors aboard Marblehead's fishing ships and merchant vessels. One of the most famous and feared pirates of all was Ned Low. He was a cruel and evil man and tales of his atrocities, even if exaggerated, struck terror in the hearts of all who heard them. His crew was drunken, disorderly and cruel. They plundered and killed their way up and down the East Coast of the American colonies, seemingly unstoppable. Ned Low had been working the waters off Nova Scotia, plucking fishing vessels and merchant ships, and had already taken twelve vessels when he came upon the fishing schooner *Mary*, owned by Joseph Doliber of Marblehead. It was a Sunday morning, and by tradition the vessels known as "Sunday keepers" did not work. The pirate ship sailed close and captured and boarded the ship. The prize that Ned Low sought this time was men for his crew, which needed to be replenished now and then. Because of his awful reputation, Low didn't get too many volunteers. One particularly grisly story about Low was that he cut off the ears of one of his captives, seasoned them with salt and pepper and forced the man to eat his own flesh. It's no wonder that very few willingly joined his crew.

Low had one peculiarity when it came to taking crew members. Though he had no qualms about killing men who were fathers of young children at home, he would not take them as crew members. He generally released them in a discarded ship to find their own way home. It was said that Ned Low himself had a daughter in Boston, but because of his reputation and the price on his head he could never return there to see her. So he spared other fathers from this terrible fate. This is probably about as close as he ever came to being humane.

Once the *Mary* was captured and renamed the *Fancy*, Low took charge of the vessel. He released most of the crew and sent them off in his discarded ship. The six single men from the *Mary*'s crew were given a choice: they could either become pirates or die. Ned Low presented this as an invitation, and all accepted. It was not an invitation that it was advisable to refuse. Philip Ashton was one of the six men, and his story is remarkable.

There were many stories of men who had been captured by pirates. Some became pirates themselves and liked the life. Some lived, some died in battles and many were uncooperative and tried to escape or were so troublesome that they were marooned on deserted islands. The novel *Robinson Crusoe* by Daniel Defoe was written after the author read true accounts of a marooned seaman. Robinson Crusoe was a fictional character, but his story was real. Philip Ashton was Marblehead's own Robinson Crusoe.

Philip Ashton was nineteen years old in 1722 when he was captured. He had no desire to be a pirate, but he did not want to die either, so he bided his time and did as he was told. He joined the pirate crew and waited for a chance to escape. For a long while no opportunity came his way. Philip was an unwilling pirate for about eight months. He worried constantly about being killed by Ned Low or being hanged as a pirate if the ship was captured. By this time the ship had made its way south into Caribbean waters.

One day the ship stopped at a small island to take on fresh water. Several men were to be sent ashore to fill and bring back wooden kegs with water. Philip Ashton volunteered to be among them. The men rowed to the island and went to look for a natural spring. Philip waited for his opportunity, and as soon as he could he ran away from the group. He hid in the jungle and managed to avoid being caught. The men searched for him for a long time, but finally had to return to the ship. Ned Low was furious that a captive had escaped. The ship sailed back and forth and all around the island for five days, hoping to catch sight of and fire on Philip Ashton. He remained hidden and finally the ship sailed away. Captain Ned Low angrily cursed Ashton. The evil pirate took some consolation from the fact that though he may have escaped, Ashton was marooned—doomed to die of starvation as he went mad with loneliness.

Such could easily have been Philip Ashton's fate. Once the excitement of being free wore off, Ashton realized he was not in great shape. He had a hard time on the island. He did have fresh water and fruits to eat. But he had no weapon and no fire to cook food or to keep him warm or as a way to signal to other ships. His feet were cut and bleeding. As did most seamen, he went barefoot onboard ship and had not brought along any shoes to go ashore. Running over shells and rocks on the island to escape the pirates had cut his feet badly. His feet were sore and some of his wounds became infected. For a while he was sick and feverish. During this time Ashton became confused, lost track of time and was very low in spirit.

After nine months alone, Philip Ashton had a visitor. A man came by canoe to the island. He was a Spaniard who made his living traveling among these small islands, bartering and trading with both white men and natives. Philip Ashton never knew his name. The man stayed for a few days and when he left he gave Ashton a knife and a powder and flint to make fires, and promised to return. He never did. Whether the man was lost in a storm at sea or never intended to return is unknown. But Ashton was in a much better condition after his visitor left, for now he could hunt for fish and cook his food. His luck really improved when he found a canoe on the other side of the island. His wounds had healed and he could explore and observe his surroundings. Ashton took his small canoe and traveled to several small islands nearby. He saw some other ships and men, but kept away from them, fearing that they were pirates. Finally he landed at the island of Roatan. Ashton stayed there alone for seven months. Then in June of 1724, two large canoes of men came to the island. Ashton watched silently until he decided that these men were not pirates and he came out of hiding. The sailors were startled and amazed by Ashton's appearance. His clothing was almost gone, his hair and beard were long and unkempt and his voice was hoarse from lack of speaking. But the men rescued him and took him with them. They listened with great curiosity to Ashton's story, asking many questions. They kept him safe until they met up with two men from a ship bound for Salem.

Philip Ashton signed on to the ship and worked his passage home to Marblehead. He arrived two years, ten months and fifteen days after he had been captured by pirates. His family was amazed and delighted, and it was as if he had come back from the dead. The whole town of Marblehead was fascinated by the story, and Parson John Barnard helped Ashton to tell the tale, writing and publishing a book in 1723 called *The Strange Adventures and Deliverances of Philip Ashton of Marblehead*. The book is an early version of the "as told to" genre. His book was quite successful, as many people were interested in life aboard a pirate vessel and the account of a truly miraculous escape.

Chapter 4.

Marblehead and the American Revolution

As Marblehead's reputation and importance as a major port for the production and trade of salted fish increased, so did its population. In the first half of the eighteenth century, Marblehead grew tremendously. Merchants took charge of their own fate, selling salted cod directly to the market, which eliminated the fees and profits of middlemen and earned the merchants a much higher profit. This was due in large part to Parson John Barnard, a young man trained in theology at Harvard College. It has been said of him that if he lived today he would have had a MBA instead of becoming a minister.

John Barnard came to Marblehead in the early 1700s and quickly assessed the financial situation. He had new ideas and felt the timing was right to expand the fishing trade and let Marblehead merchants take control of their own product. Under his guidance local merchants were persuaded to take a risk and strike out on their own. He convinced Joseph Swett to try selling salted fish in Barbados himself, rather than through an agent. Swett's resulting profits were high, and his example set the stage for the prosperity that Marblehead began to enjoy. A winning combination was already in place with Marblehead's deep harbor, experienced fishermen and an efficient salt-fish processing system. Everyone benefited.

Tucker's Wharf on Marblehead Harbor, lithograph. *Illustration from* Nooks and Corners of New England, *S.A. Drake, 1875.*

Increased trade soon led to a new form of vessel as well, a fishing schooner that was larger, heavier and better able to travel long distances. It was called the Marblehead Heeltapper because of its shape. It looked like an upside down shoe afloat. The name Heeltapper was also a reference to the shoemaking sideline that many Marblehead fishermen used as a way to supplement their incomes.

The town of Marblehead began to change as a result of this newfound wealth. Merchants with increased income built or remodeled their property into more elegant homes, mostly in the English Georgian style. Luxury goods were included in returning ships, providing the "codfish aristocracy" with English porcelain tea sets, mirrors, silks and fine linens, fireplace tiles and pianos. As an English colony, Massachusetts looked to London as the source of style and culture. Engravings of English fashion, known as fashion plates, as well as architectural plans and furniture styles and patterns, made their way to Marblehead and to all the

New England colonies. The colonies became prosperous, and the standard of living improved steadily. In the years leading up to the American Revolution, Marblehead became one of the ten most affluent towns in the colonies.

Jeremiah Lee and His Mansion

In the 1720s and '30s many men were attracted to Marblehead because of opportunities that seemed on the rise. Among them was a young man named Jeremiah Lee. He and his father came from Manchester on Cape Ann, a town a little farther north of Marblehead. They saw possibilities for money to be made and took advantage of them. Lee began by supplying ships for ocean voyages as a shoreman, the predecessors of longshoremen, who still are responsible for loading and unloading vessels all over the world. Then he began buying ships. He also married well, choosing as his bride Martha Swett, daughter of Joseph Swett, the daring and successful early merchant trader. Lee's financial success grew until he became without question the wealthiest man in Marblehead, and arguably the richest man in the American colonies.

As his wealth grew, Lee had a desire to build for himself and his family a fabulous mansion. Many prosperous colonists did the same, though few of these impressive mansions remain. Lee found his spot on what was to become Washington Street in Marblehead. He purchased several houses, tore them down and began construction on the Lee Mansion. It was built following English Georgian architectural plans, and is a classic Georgian home of elegant proportions, with a center entrance framed by a Greek columned portico, a massive Palladian-influenced window at the stair landing and a double-wide hall and staircase. No expense was spared in the embellishments of the house, and colonial master craftsmen showed their skill in carved mahogany rosettes and a grand staircase as well as a Baroque fruit and floral mantel and over mantel in the great hall. Hand-painted wallpaper was ordered from paperstainers in London, with classical Greco Roman designs in the hall and stairway, pastoral scenes in one upstairs bedroom and maritime scenes in another. Hand-blocked wallpaper was chosen for most of the other rooms. Fireplace tiles were ordered from Messrs. Sadler and Green in London, and furniture was made by cabinetmakers in Boston and the North Shore. Completed in 1768, the Lee Mansion has been a showplace from the day it was completed until the present, and a source of pride for Lee and the whole town of Marblehead. Jeremiah and Martha Lee moved in with five of their six children. Their eldest son had just left to attend Harvard College, which was essentially the only college available at the time.

Jeremiah Lee had been active in Marblehead town affairs from the time he arrived, was colonel of a Marblehead militia, represented the town on various committees and generally took an active role in civic matters. He was clearly an intelligent and involved citizen. As the years that led up to the American Revolution progressed, his feelings about independence became more pronounced, as did those of many colonists.

The causes of the American Revolution are complex, and the events leading to the war are as involved as those leading to any war. But the growing wealth and success of the colonies, based on a sense of self-reliance and freedom from governmental constraint, created an attitude of independence. It was this attitude that caused colonists to increasingly rebel against forms of taxation and restricted freedom that they felt to be unfair. England, financially strained by years of European wars, sought more and more income from the American colonies. They were such a rich prize, waiting to be plucked. Perhaps if the Crown had been less greedy, and more willing to extend self-governing rights, an open break would not have occurred.

Jeremiah Lee was, and remains, a man of mystery for a variety of reasons. His name appears in various town records, and he was on a committee with Elbridge Gerry, Azor Orne and other Marbleheaders known to be sympathetic to the patriotic cause. But no letters or personal papers of any sort have survived. The story of his death is both tragic and perplexing. Jeremiah Lee had probably been using his ships to smuggle weapons into the colonies in direct defiance of embargos aimed at keeping the colonists' supply of arms to a minimum. Lee had been helping the patriotic cause by transporting gunpowder and weapons. Once these goods arrived in Marblehead they were conveyed to Concord in hogshead barrels labeled "Fish." On April 18, 1775, the same night that Paul Revere rode to every village and town, Lee attended a meeting in a tavern in Menotomy, now Lexington, with Samuel Adams and John Hancock. They stayed overnight and finally heard the Redcoats coming, searching house to house for traitors. John Hancock in particular was a well-known target, but they were all involved in treasonous activity, so they ran from the inn in their nightclothes and hid in the surrounding cornfields to avoid being taken. Of course the next morning the war

The Lee Mansion, lithograph. *Illustration from* Nooks and Corners of New England, *S.A. Drake, 1875.*

was launched with the "shot heard 'round the world," Lexington and Concord became forever famous and the American Revolution had begun. But the night in the fields had been as fatal as a bullet for Jeremiah Lee. He caught his death of cold, quite literally, developed pneumonia and died three weeks later. He never came home to Marblehead. He was taken up the Charles River to a farm in Newbury apparently owned by him or a family connection and was nursed there, without success. Mrs. Lee was left a widow, and the Lee fortune was in a precarious state. Lee's twenty-two ships were mostly at sea when war was declared and it took thirteen years for his estate to be settled.

But why are there no records of Lee's affairs? What happened to his papers, his letters, journals and other personal accounts? There is nothing but a few account books remaining of the records of this prominent and patriotic multimillionaire.

A psychic who visited the Lee Mansion in the 1970s had a vision of Martha Lee sitting beside the fire in her upstairs parlor burning piles of papers. Is that true? Since Lee knew that he was engaged in treasonous activities, would he have warned his wife to destroy everything if anything happened to him? It certainly is possible. Yet it is tempting to hope that somehow, somewhere a hidden chest remains that could hold answers to the many questions about Lee and his and other Marblehead Patriots' roles in the American Revolution.

Tories

Jeremiah Lee's story represents one side of the reaction to British control of the American colonies. The more common response for most wealthy merchants was to want to preserve the status quo. This was true throughout the colonies, and Marblehead was no exception.

When the Second Continental Congress met in Philadelphia in 1775 and named George Washington as leader of the army, it became clear that decisions as to loyalty had to be made. Although the popular myth is that all American colonists rallied around the cause for freedom and independence, the reality was quite different. There were many who wanted to find a compromise and wished to avoid war. For as many reasons as men wanted war, there were also many reasons to oppose it. In Marblehead, most members of St. Michael's Church, the Church of England, were against the war. Seen as a bastion of dissent, the Church of England was outlawed by the Continental Congress, and St. Michael's was ordered to be closed. British sympathizers, or Tories, became the enemy as well as the British themselves. Giving aid or supplies to the British troops was forbidden and known Tories began to be arrested.

As sentiments escalated and the war began, it became increasingly difficult for Tories to continue their lives in the colonies. Many returned to England or fled to Canada. When a Tory took refuge in the home of Mrs. Bowden of Marblehead, angry citizens pounded on her door and demanded that she give him up. She answered the door and said, "Gentlemen, I assure you that the man you seek is not under this roof!" She did not lie. The escaping man was up on the roof, hiding behind the chimney.

Some wealthy merchants were unwilling to give up their property and tried to hold out. In Marblehead, Thomas Robie was one. He had made enemies by overtly opposing separation from England. He and his family made their disdain for the cause of freedom well known. By 1775 they could hold out no longer, and left Marblehead for Halifax, Nova Scotia. They sailed from the town landing, where an angry mob had gathered to see them off with jeers and taunts. Mrs. Robie was incensed and told the crowd, "I hope that I shall live to return, find this wicked rebellion crushed and see the streets of Marblehead so deep in Rebel blood that a long boat might be rowed through them." The Robies and many other Tories eventually did return to Marblehead, but when they did it was as citizens of a new republic.

King Hooper, one of the most successful of Marblehead's merchant traders in the years before the Revolution, was also driven out of town. He was Jeremiah Lee's brother-in-law, and had made a huge fortune in the salted cod trade. Older than Lee, Hooper was considered the first "king" of the trade. He was very well liked for his fair dealings and generosity in the provisioning of his ships. He always made sure there was an ample supply of food and water for the voyages, and that they were of high quality. He remodeled his father's small seventeenth-century house into an imposing Georgian mansion, building onto the existing house so that examples of both seventeenth- and eighteenth-century style still coexist in the house on Hooper Street. Hooper added parlors, a staircase and two additional floors to the original house. The top floor is an elegantly appointed ballroom with a sprung floor designed for dancing. It was the first of its kind in Marblehead, and was the scene of many a beautiful candlelit ball. But all his prosperity and popularity couldn't protect King Hooper from the desire for independence and the emotions that it let loose. He finally left town, headed, as many other Loyalists, for the Canadian Maritime Provinces. Hooper also eventually returned to Marblehead, but he never regained either his wealth or his popularity.

The American Revolution has many tales of daring and sacrifice that led to the creation of a new form of government. But the story has another side as well, of colonists who wanted to stay loyal to the

English king and protect what they had worked for under what they felt was a satisfactory form of government.

Marblehead Privateer: Captain Mugford

The story of James Mugford of Marblehead is a hero's saga. Mugford was a respected ship captain at a young age. His voyages were successful and he made many trips across the Atlantic. In the 1770s, however, the voyage became increasingly dangerous for colonial vessels because of the risk of impressment by the British navy. The British were always on the lookout for more men to serve in their navy. It was a poorly paid, difficult and undesirable job. To add to their numbers the British navy often captured merchant ships and impressed some or all of the crew members into service. Many colonial crews were captured and the practice was deeply resented. This happened to Mugford just before the start of the American Revolution, when his ship was overtaken and the entire crew was forced to serve in the British navy against their will. During his time of enforced service on a British ship, Mugford began to hear rumors and stories of a "powder ship" full of ammunition that was scheduled to leave England headed for the American colonies. He realized the significance of this cargo, its potentially devastating effects for the struggling Patriots, who were already short of ammunition, and the huge advantage to the British troops if the "powder ship" reached its destination.

Not long after hearing this rumor, Mugford was finally released from his service in the British navy, and he headed back to the colonies as fast as possible. Once there he requested permission to be authorized as a privateer and to use his ship, the *Franklin*, to capture the "powder ship" named the *Hope*. He was duly authorized and set out in search of his prize.

Mugford was aboard the *Franklin* when he came upon the *Hope* heading toward Boston Harbor. His vessel was much smaller than the *Hope* but he used her to great advantage. He soon overtook the *Hope*, boarded her and captured the crew. Then he forced the ship into a tidal inlet, where she was grounded in the low tide. Once the ship was immobile, the sea was suddenly full of every kind of small vessel available to Patriots along the shore. They had all gotten word of the "powder ship" and its capture and they quickly went into action to unload all the precious gunpowder as well as any other tools and weapons they could find. Soon the ship was stripped of everything and

[The above is the Effigy of the truly brave and heroic Captain JAMES MUGFORD, Junior, late Commander of the Franklin Privateer Schooner, lately fitted out from Marblehead, mounting a few two pounders and fwivels, and manned with twenty-one men, who on the feventeenth of May, 1776, valiantly attacked and took a King's Store-fhip, of about three hundred tons burthen, bound from Cork to Bofton, mounting fix carriage guns, befides fwivels, and manned with eighteen men, which is efteemed the richeft prize that has been brought into any port in the American Colonies fince the commencement of the war, having on board fifteen hundred barrels of powder, defigned for the ufe of our cruel and implacable enemies, the Britifh fleet and army, employed to enflave the Continent:——This intrepid and gallant HERO, moft unfortunately for his Country, fell a facrifice in defence of its juft RIGHTS and LIBERTIES, on the nineteenth of the fame May, in a defperate engagement with thirteen boats, manned with two hundred failors from the Britifh fleet.

Effigy of the Truly Brave and Heroic Captain James Mugford, Junior, late Commander of the Franklin Privateer Schooner, woodblock printed broadside, circa 1776. *Courtesy of the Marblehead Museum & Historical Society.*

anything that could be of use. It was a great prize, and a great boost to the patriotic cause.

When the *Franklin* set out to sea again, she tragically became a victim of the same low tide. She too was caught by the combination of a narrow passage and not enough sea to float her. British vessels in the area soon realized their advantage and moved in to take their revenge. The Marblehead crew fought back with all their strength and a vicious battle ensued. Captain Mugford was shot by British cannon fire and fell to the deck of the *Franklin*. Mortally wounded and aware that he was dying, Mugford urged his men to keep fighting and save the ship. The crew rallied and fought on, and finally the tide turned in their favor and the *Franklin* was free.

The ship was able to sail back to Marblehead Harbor. The shore and the docks were full of townspeople waiting to celebrate this exciting victory. Mugford's young wife was taken out to the *Franklin*, where she held her dying husband in her arms and kissed him goodbye. Marblehead mourned his loss and rejoiced in the bravery of one of their own. He was then and is still considered a hero. A monument to the brave and daring young Captain James Mugford was erected and still stands on Old Burial Hill.

Glover's Regiment

As the war began, Marblehead men began to enlist in the local regiments. The day before the Battle of Bunker Hill, Colonel John Glover was made head of the Twenty-first Regiment and was ordered to stay in Marblehead to gather men and defend the town. Another Marblehead company, led by Captain Sam Trevett, answered the call and marched to Boston, where they fought at the Battle of Bunker Hill and two Marblehead men died. A few days later Glover's regiment, with over four hundred men, left Marblehead to begin what was an amazing story of courage and determination that genuinely shaped the course of the war.

During the Revolution, John Glover of Marblehead and his regiment of fishermen were highly valued by General George Washington and helped carry out several major military maneuvers by water. The crossing of the Delaware River on Christmas night, 1776, to attack the Hessian mercenaries of the British army in Trenton marked the first victory of the Revolution. It could not have been accomplished without Glover's men and their seafaring abilities. They knew how to row, how to handle the boats they confiscated for the task and they had the strength, skill and determination to transport 2,400 men plus horses and artillery across a river filled with chunks of ice. They traveled tirelessly back and forth through the icy water all night long until all the troops finally were on the New Jersey side of the river.

The famous painting *Washington Crossing the Delaware* by Emmanuel Gottlieb Leutze, made almost one hundred years after the event, remains a source of frustration to the people of Marblehead. Painted in a heroic and monumental style, the artist's composition is concerned with making a strong statement of the significance of the event. Washington is shown standing nobly in the bow of the boat. Given the conditions of weather and the limited stability of such a small vessel, this would have been highly unlikely. If Washington had tried to stand, John Glover certainly would have put him in his place, literally and figuratively. Glover was a feisty man who was a good leader, always concerned for the safety of his crew. He was outspoken, and known to have tried Washington's patience many times. He would not have allowed Washington to risk either his own life or that of his men by foolishly standing up. So though Marbleheaders are justifiably proud of the event and of Glover and his regiment, they cannot look at the painting without cringing.

General John Glover and his regiment became legends, and their heroism is a source of great pride to the people of Marblehead. Glover's Regiment still exists as a group of dedicated reenactors who regularly appear in parades and at almost all town events. They dress as the regiment did, mostly in the clothes of common seamen. They carry an assortment of weapons that they provide themselves, and portray or reenact a variety of personalities and interests.

Fort Sewall's Defense

Money and resources needed by the Revolutionary army had left many coastal towns without adequate men and arms to defend themselves. Fort Sewall, established in the 1600s as the site of a natural defense of Marblehead's harbor and town, was in sad shape. The fort had few cannon and virtually no ammunition. The fort itself was in poor repair. The town had petitioned for money to remedy this but it was slow in coming.

The threat of British warships was increasing and soon several British naval vessels, including the *Lively* and the *Nautilus*, were sighted

Fort Sewall, nineteenth-century lithograph. *Courtesy of the Marblehead Museum & Historical Society.*

just outside of Marblehead Harbor. There was cause for panic, as there were few men to fight, but Marbleheaders kept their heads and came up with a plan. Women and children were evacuated and the men set to work at Fort Sewall. They aimed the cannons toward the British ships to make it appear that entering ships would be shot. They assembled every available man on the ramparts, even those too old or too young, and looked ready to fight. They stood in battle position and stared the enemy down.

It was all a complete hoax. There was no ammunition to fire the cannon, and not enough men to defend the town. It was a bluff, but it worked. The British navy backed down and sailed away to find a town with less defense that they could easily overtake. They never knew that what they had witnessed was an act created to cover the truth. Quick thinking and ingenuity by the people of Marblehead saved the day.

Birthplace of the American Navy?

As the Revolutionary War began, it became increasingly evident that this "people's war" was underfunded and had very few of the supplies

Portrait of Elbridge Gerry, after an engraving. *Illustration from* Nooks and Corners of New England, *S.A. Drake, 1875.*

necessary to carry out a war. Guns, ammunition and saltpeter had been restricted as imports by the British in the years leading up to the war. Now their shortage was critical, and their lack was a serious detriment to the Patriots' ability to fight. Elbridge Gerry of Marblehead, known as "the signer" because he signed the Declaration of Independence, was a Patriot who spent his life before, during and after the Revolution working for an independent nation. He realized the vital importance and need for these supplies. He urged George Washington to stockpile them and suggested that armed privateers be used to capture British vessels and steal their ammunition.

John Glover was authorized to find merchant vessels, arm them and send them out as legalized privateers. The first vessel was one of Glover's ships, the *Hannah*, a seaworthy West Indies trader. Marbleheader Nicholas Broughton became her captain and the crew was mostly from Marblehead as well. The ship was outfitted as a vessel of war at Beverly, provided with cannons for attack and defense. She went to sea as the first ship of the Revolutionary War's navy in September of 1775.

The *Hannah*'s naval career was short and not very successful, but that hasn't stopped an ongoing fascination with her. On her first voyage the *Hannah* was chased by the Royal Navy vessel the *Lively*, which had harassed the Marblehead coast for years. On her second voyage the *Hannah* was attacked by the *Nautilus*, a British ship that had orders to burn her. Most accounts state that the *Hannah* was destroyed, or at least damaged beyond repair. There is, however, another version that claims the *Hannah* was secretly rebuilt and renamed the *Lynch*. She reportedly went back to fight in 1776 and redeemed her reputation.

There are no actual contemporary paintings or drawings of the *Hannah*, though many imaginary ones exist. The right to claim the first ship in the American navy is an ongoing feud. Both Marblehead and Beverly call themselves the "birthplace of the American navy." And they are not the only ones. Several other locations also claim the title. Each place has its own reason and story. For Marblehead, there will always be only one ship. The *Hannah*, though once a real ship, has taken on mythical proportions in a misty past of unrealized maritime victories.

George Washington in Marblehead

General George Washington was a man truly beloved during his lifetime. The title of "Father of his Country" was bestowed because of his actions. Washington wanted to be president, rather than king of the new United States, so that he could guide and support the cause of independence. When Washington became president he was grateful and appreciative of all the men who had fought beside him during the many dark days of the Revolution. He felt a bond particularly with some of his generals, who knew, as he did, how many times the whole cause was on the brink of ruin.

One man to whom he felt particularly grateful was General John Glover. Glover had saved the Continental army several times. He was opinionated and sometimes disagreeable, but he was honest and brave and he rose to Washington's challenges each time he was asked. He in his turn respected Washington as a military genius. He might have doubted the possibility of coveying 2,400 men across the Delaware River in the dark of night, but he knew that as a military plan it was brilliant. So he applied himself and his regiment to the challenge, and they succeeded.

In 1789 President Washington made a triumphal tour of the country, visiting cities and towns and meeting with his supporters. Washington insisted on coming to Marblehead. He was scheduled to visit Salem and he wanted to go to Marblehead as well.

When the board of selectmen, the governing body that has guided the town since the 1600s, found out that President Washington was coming to Marblehead they began immediately to make plans for his visit. Speeches were written and a parade was planned. Martha Lee, widow of Jeremiah, was asked if President Washington could be entertained at the grandest house in town, the Lee Mansion. Of course she agreed. Washington was welcomed on the steps of the Old Town House, and everyone in town came out to greet him. Speeches were delivered and then, accompanied by music and songs, the entire crowd marched down the street to the Lee Mansion along the newly named Washington Street. They entered the house, were greeted by Mrs. Lee and were served tea and "cold collations" in the great hall. There are few possessions of the Lee family remaining in the Lee Mansion today, but the dining room chairs are from the original house and it is intriguing to wonder on which of these George Washington may have sat.

The Lafayette House

The Marquis de Lafayette was just twenty-one years old when he became interested in and began to support the American Revolution in 1777. He was a French nobleman, and the heir to a grand title and a large fortune. He was an orphan at the age of thirteen and married by the time he was sixteen. Lafayette was not particularly interested in life at the court of Louis XVI. What he was intrigued with were the efforts of the American colonies to free themselves from British rule. He traveled to America and offered his support to the cause.

At first the Continental Congress was suspicious of Lafayette. He persisted, and his straightforward offer to serve the patriotic cause finally won them over. Lafayette wanted to serve in the army, and he was assigned to General George Washington. They became lifelong friends, and as they were more like father and son in age, that was the essence of their relationship. Lafayette served the Patriots well as a commander, a supporter and a financier. He was devoted to the cause of freedom. He was wounded in action, but he continued to fight. Lafayette was charming, intelligent and very well liked. He made many friends in the colonies. At the end of the Revolution, just after Cornwallis surrendered at Yorktown, Lafayette returned to France.

He stayed in contact with Washington, and three years later when President Washington invited Lafayette to visit the new United States, he accepted with great pleasure. He was greeted with parades, honored at dinner and balls and generally fêted as he traveled through the former colonies. He came to Boston, where he was welcomed with open arms. He wanted to visit Marblehead, and when he arrived he was greeted with speeches, celebrations and a grand dinner. His reaction and response to the people of Marblehead is recorded in a letter he wrote that now is owned by the town of Marblehead. Lafayette's compassion and spirit are evident in this excerpt: "Amidst our regrets of brave men who had the honor to fall in their country's cause, I rejoice in the virtuous spirit and animating industry remarkable in the remaining sons of Marblehead."

Lafayette was glad to see his old friend General John Glover and was entertained at the home of Elbridge Gerry, the ardent Patriot from Marblehead who went on to become vice-president of the United States under James Madison. At the dinner party, according to custom, thirteen toasts were drunk in honor of the original thirteen colonies. On this visit, Lafayette stayed just one night, leaving to continue on his triumphal tour.

Forty years later, in 1824, the Marquis de Lafayette returned to the United States. He was sixty-seven years old and still enormously popular. Once again he was greeted with ceremonies and parades, dinners and balls. When he arrived in the nation's new capital, Washington, D.C., Lafayette was greeted by twenty-four young ladies dressed in red, white and blue, each one bearing a shield of the nation's twenty-four states. He made his way back to Marblehead, and arrived in August 1824 to great fanfare. He was as eagerly and warmly welcomed as

Sun, detail from an eighteenth-century Chinese export porcelain bowl. *Courtesy of the Marblehead Museum & Historical Society.*

he had been on his first visit. He dined at the Lee Mansion, owned at that time by the Bank of Marblehead. It was still considered the grandest house in town, and worthy of entertaining such a honored and beloved guest. Lafayette's visit to the New World must have been somewhat bittersweet, as many of his companions from Revolutionary War times were gone. George Washington, Elbridge Gerry and John Glover were all dead. But he was happy to see the strength and energy of the new Republic stronger than ever. Lafayette had brought his son, George Washington Lafayette, to America with him. When they came to Marblehead they both visited Mary Glover Hooper, the daughter of John Glover. This event was appreciated by the whole town and remembered fondly by Mrs. Hooper herself. She gave the dress she wore to dance with Lafayette to the Marblehead Historical Society to preserve her memories of that day.

Lafayette's visit forms the basis of one of the most frequently told Marblehead myths. At the corner of Hooper Street, a total of five small streets come together to form an intersection. A house at this corner is known as the Lafayette house. The story goes that on Lafayette's second visit to Marblehead he arrived in a large and beautiful coach pulled by six white horses. He rode in his carriage around the streets of Marblehead as a part of his welcome. It is frequently recorded that it was a rainy day and of course the streets were slippery with mud. As the procession made its way up the steep hill that leads from the harbor, Lafayette's carriage was unable to make the turn onto Hooper Street. Someone in the procession decided to chop away part of the house that was in the way, thereby making it possible for Lafayette and his admirers to continue their parade. To this day the left corner of the house is missing.

This story is told over and over. But on consideration it seems unlikely. Was there no other solution to the problem? Didn't the homeowner object when someone started sawing and chopping away at his house? This myth is intriguing because it raises so many questions. It is so ingrained that it seems likely that there *is* some connection between Lafayette's visit and this house. Though the whole story is not true, some part of it may be. There are some other explanations about why part of the house is missing. It has been said that it was a candy shop, apparently for drive-by treats, though no other shops were built in this format. It is a very steep hill, and was a common route from the harbor to the center of town. Certainly many wagons and carriages came up and down this hill, and it is a narrow turn. Perhaps the house was built or remodeled like this to accommodate them. Whatever the reasons, the house will forever be the Lafayette house, and the story will always be told as a reminder of the famous visits of the Marquis de Lafayette to the town of Marblehead. This legend is too well loved to ever give in to logic.

Chapter 5.

The Nineteenth Century War and Fishing

In 1761 Marblehead had been a wealthy town with an active port. The end of the Revolutionary War left the town's fishing fleet and its economy in ruins. Personal fortunes were destroyed and many of the wealthiest men had nothing left. The whole town rejoiced in the new United States, but financially it suffered. Ships, men and the economy were gone. Many men were dead, others imprisoned. It would be years before the fate of some of them was known. Like the rest of the country, Marblehead struggled to rebuild, regroup and move forward.

The Embargo Act of 1807 stalled the fishing fleets again, and the struggle to regain lost prosperity continued. Fishing was the main occupation of most men in Marblehead, and those who didn't fish had jobs related to the trade. What happened at sea was of vital importance to everyone.

Skipper Ireson's Ride

In the fall of 1808 the *Betty*, a Marblehead fishing schooner, was on a homeward-bound voyage. The night was stormy and the seas were rough. The *Betty* was hailed by a ship in distress, the fishing schooner *Active*. Skipper Floyd Ireson did not answer the call, nor did he lay by

Unloading Fish at Marblehead. Engraving from Nooks and Corners of New England, *S.A. Drake, 1875.*

the ship until morning, as was a common practice in high seas when rescue was impossible. The *Betty* sailed on home to Marblehead. When the ship had docked the crew made their way to the local tavern and told their version of the story. Townsfolk were horrified, as the account violated every unwritten law of the sea. To leave fellow mariners in distress, without even a gesture toward helping them, was the worst crime imaginable.

The next night a crowd of men and women appeared at Skipper Ireson's house. He lived at 19 Circle Street, in a house that still attracts visitors. The fishermen of Marblehead and their wives and families were incensed at "Flud" Ireson's behavior. They grabbed him and proceeded to tar and feather him. This process is often described in a humorous way, but in fact it was a cruel and painful process. Boiling hot tar burned the skin, and the chicken feathers had sharp quills that pierced the burned flesh. Once Skipper Ireson was tarred and feathered he was placed in an old dory and dragged through the streets of Marblehead. Townsfolk came out to cheer the action and to jeer at the skipper. The crowd and the dory were halted by Salem constables as they came down the hill from Marblehead into Salem.

1. Carved and painted codfish, **J.O.J.** Frost, house paint on wood, circa 1920s. *Courtesy of the Marblehead Museum & Historical Society.*

2. *Fishing Schooners in Marblehead Harbor*, artist unknown, fireboard, circa 1720s. *Courtesy of the Marblehead Museum & Historical Society.*

3. Marblehead Harbor, from the journals of Ashley Bowen. Dated 1763, this is believed to be the earliest view of the town. *Courtesy of the Marblehead Museum & Historical Society.*

4. Pirate's treasure. *Photograph by Marcia Hunkins, 2007; courtesy of the Marblehead Museum & Historical Society.*

5. *Marblehead Harbor by Moonlight. Illustration from* Rudder Magazine, *1912.*

6. Marblehead sampler by Polly Ellis, dated 1791. *Courtesy of the Marblehead Museum &*
Historical Society.

7. *Portrait of John Glover*, ink and gouache on ivory, miniature, circa 1760s. *Courtesy of the Marblehead Museum & Historical Society.*

8. *The Apotheosis of George Washington*, eglomise or reverse glass painting, Chinese export, circa 1820s. *Courtesy of the Marblehead Museum & Historical Society.*

9. *Portrait of Jeremiah Lee*, John Singleton Copley, oil on canvas, circa 1768. *Courtesy of the Wadsworth Athenaeum, Hartford, Connecticut.*

10. *Bird's Eye View of Marblehead*, J.O.J. Frost, house paint on wall board, circa 1920s.
Courtesy of the Marblehead Museum & Historical Society.

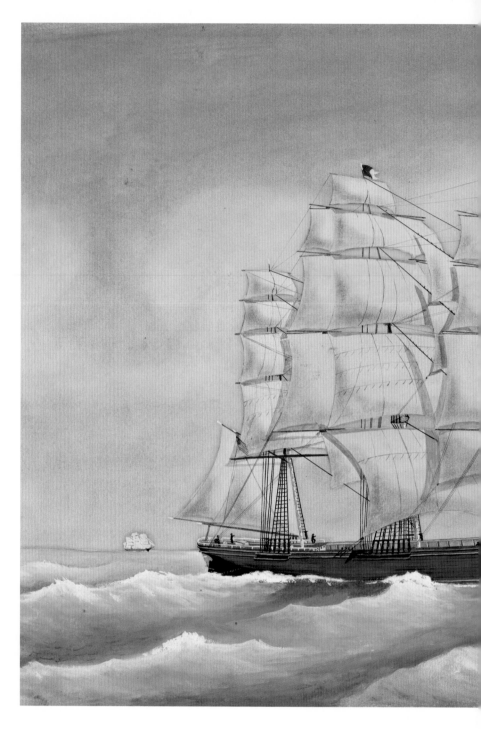

11. *The Flying Cloud*, John F. Leavitt, watercolor, circa 1920s. *Courtesy of the Marblehead Museum & Historical Society.*

12. *Pigs Being Driven to Market Along Washington Street,* J.O.J. Frost, house paint on wall board, circa 1920s. *Courtesy of the Marblehead Museum & Historical Society.*

THE OLD BRUCE
HOUSE

J.O.J.FROST

GS FOR
SALE

13. *Postcard of Artist by the Seaside*, advertising postcard, nineteenth century. *Courtesy of the Marblehead Museum & Historical Society.*

14. *Looking Toward the Harbor,* Frank Butler, colored woodcut, circa 1940s. *Courtesy of the Marblehead Museum & Historical Society.*

15. *Marblehead Harbor*, C.H. Snow, watercolor, circa 1920s. *Private collection.*

16. *Marblehead Coast*, John Joseph Enneking, oil on canvas, late nineteenth century. *Courtesy of the Marblehead Museum & Historical Society.*

Ireson's House, Oakum Bay, Marblehead, lithograph. *Illustration from* Nooks and Corners of New England, *S.A. Drake, 1875.*

Skipper Ireson was released and sent home, but his career as a ship's captain was over. He ended his life selling fish from a cart.

Years later, John Greenleaf Whittier heard the story. He made it into an epic ballad, published as "Skipper Ireson's Ride" in 1857.

> *The strangest ride that ever was sped,*
> *Was Ireson's out of Marblehead!*
> *Old Floyd Ireson, for his hard heart,*
> *Tarred and feathered and carried in a cart,*
> *By the women of Marblehead.*

By the time this poem was printed and circulated, Skipper Ireson was dead. He had always claimed that he had wanted to stop to help the distressed ship, but his crew refused. But whatever the truth, it was an embarrassment for Marblehead. The town historian, Samuel Roads Jr. recorded Ireson's version in his book, *The History and Traditions of Marblehead*, and also wrote a letter to Whittier explaining Ireson's claims. Whittier sent a letter of apology. Whatever happened onboard the *Betty* that night is unknown, but the story lives on, as does Skipper Ireson's infamy.

"Old Ironsides" and the War of 1812

The War of 1812 was an unpopular war in Marblehead. Once more merchant ships and fishing sloops were hindered from going about their business. Ships were seized by the British and men were imprisoned. The town struggled with poverty and gave what it could to poor fishermen's families. The fort at the mouth of the harbor was reinforced and rearmed once again, and the threat from the sea was constant.

On April 13, 1814, the town watched a dramatic display of seamanship unfold before their eyes. The USS *Constitution*, an American naval vessel that had already earned itself the nickname "Old Ironsides" when cannon shot bounced off her hull, was being chased by two British frigates, *Tenedos* and *Junon*. Both of these ships were very well armed and had more cannon than the *Constitution*. They had her on the run, with everything working against her, including the fact that it was two against one. The *Constitution* was moving fast, dumping provisions and any extra weight overboard. But the British were gaining on her, and she needed a place to hide and regroup if she was ever to have a chance.

The *Constitution* was getting close to Marblehead Harbor, which was a possible safe refuge. But the entrance into the harbor is treacherous. Samuel Green, a member of *Constitution*'s crew and a native of Marblehead, volunteered to guide her safely into the harbor. He skillfully steered between Marblehead Rock and Marblehead Neck and into the harbor. The *Constitution* was safe. The British vessels didn't follow because they knew how difficult the passage was. They also saw ready cannons mounted at the fort by the mouth of the harbor.

The *Constitution* had performed a daring move that put the British in check, and "Old Ironsides" was saved by a seaman from Marblehead. This deed has become famous, and as the *Constitution* is now a National Landmark moored in Boston, it is often remembered. "Old Ironsides" hardly ever leaves Boston nowadays, but she made a triumphal sail in 1933 and again in 1997 and Marblehead was the place she visited. Her gratitude to the town has lasted for over 150 years.

During the War of 1812 many American ships were seized and many men were imprisoned in the notorious Dartmoor prison in England. When the war ended, the release of prisoners held there was extremely slow in coming. Hundreds of men from Marblehead were imprisoned at Dartmoor. To emphasize this there was a story told in which an English guard asked a prisoner, "Where are you from then, Jack?" "Marblehead," said the man. "Marblehead! I believe every Yankee inside these walls hails from Marblehead. It must be the greatest seaport in America! Where the devil is Marblehead?" "It's about fourteen miles from Bunker Hill," answered the Marbleheader.

Though they hadn't yet been released, the prisoners at Dartmoor became aware of the end of the war and the treaty that ensured their release. They grew restless and frustrated. The prison was overcrowded, unheated and miserable. It was surrounded by a mile of circular wall, which made escape impossible. Tension mounted and finally erupted into open revolt in the prison exercise yard. A British guard fired into the crowd of prisoners and killed nine men. Thirty-eight more were wounded, including several men from Marblehead. Reports of this incident and complaints about conditions reached home and there was tremendous pressure put on the United States government to get the men released. Finally they were free to go. The prisoners were loaded onto ships to be brought back to their homes. One of the ships carrying men from Marblehead was considered by its passengers to be going too slow. The Marbleheaders on board took control of the ship and sailed as fast as they could for home.

The end of the War of 1812 again left Marblehead in hard financial circumstances. The fishing fleet and other vessels were in poor repair, as was the harbor itself. But this time there was a strong sense of confidence and belief that the town could recover. Most Americans felt pretty cocky; they had just beaten the British for the second time in thirty-five years. Economic conditions were improving and the country stood on the verge of a huge surge of growth that swept Marblehead and the young United States into a dominant position in the world.

The Sea Serpent

Tales of sea serpents have long been told by sailors from every land and seen in every sea. In Marblehead in 1817 a sea serpent was sighted off Marblehead, out beyond the harbor near Tinker's Island. A greasy film was seen on the water where the creature had surfaced, which was cited as evidence of his appearance. A sketch was made and a description was circulated: the sea serpent was 130 feet long, measured 3 feet around and had fourteen bumps about 10 feet apart that got progressively smaller from head to tail. The creature was dark brown with a white throat and it moved slowly in an up and down

Sketch of a Sea Serpent, Sam Roads, pen and ink, July 12, 1883. *Courtesy of the Marblehead Museum & Historical Society.*

motion, except when it turned quickly like a snake. Flocks of birds followed its wake.

The sea serpent was spotted from Marblehead Neck. Fishermen searched for it with the hopes of capturing and displaying it for profit. The Eastern Stage Coach from Boston brought many weekend tourists to Marblehead hoping for a glimpse of the sea serpent. Many people claimed to have seen it, and testimonials by respectable citizens, government officials and professional men from the city were printed in the newspapers. Interest in the sea serpent, which was sighted from Lynn to Gloucester, continued throughout the nineteenth century. Repeated sightings all along the North Shore kept interest alive, and a Sea Serpent Club was formed.

In the twentieth century interest appeared to wane. Then in 1939 the sea serpent was sighted again off Marblehead. A report from Captain Albert Pierce states, "At Marblehead, lobster fishermen saw [the creature] three days after I did and reported it all around...I used to laugh when they talked about sea serpents but when I saw this one I was convinced. He was at least sixty feet long and he had fins...the water was all greasy where he went down." The description certainly seems similar to the sea serpent that was first seen in the early nineteenth century.

Even that account seems like a long time ago. Then as recently as 1997 the sea serpent was spotted again. Two men in a fishing boat reported a sighting in Fortune Bay off Newfoundland. On May 4 at about midday, they saw what they thought were garbage bags floating on the ocean's surface. They headed toward them, intending to scoop them up and dispose of them properly. They got the scare of their lives when the bags suddenly turned away, moving in a rhythmic up and down motion. A head rose up and looked at them. The fishermen described it as a head like a horse, but with eyes "like a human…he just looked at us and slid under the water and disappeared."

No one has seen a sea serpent lately, but one is sure to turn up again soon.

Captain Foster's Gold

There was a local legend that interested visitors and locals alike, all of whom wished they could solve it for their own gain. It was one of many tales told at Putnam's Tavern on the corner of Washington Street and Rockaway. The tavern is long gone, and today the site is part of the Lee Mansion gardens. But in the nineteenth century it was a popular gathering place for visitors to the town who wanted to mingle with true Marbleheaders and hear the local gossip.

A favorite topic was the story of Captain Israel Foster, owner and captain of the *Storm*. Captain Foster had prospered in trade and kept his fortune in gold pieces, preferably Spanish doubloons and English sovereigns. He kept his hoard of more than $53,000 in an old wooden keg. The War of 1812 and the threat of enemy invasion made the captain nervous, so he took his keg of gold to a bank in Salem for safe keeping. He visited the bank on occasion and took what he needed from the keg that was stored in the bank's vault. By the time Captain Foster died in 1818, he had withdrawn about $7,600.

When his heirs came to the bank to withdraw the rest, they were very surprised and not at all pleased. The remaining layer of gold pieces at the top of the barrel was not deep, and underneath it the rest of the barrel was filled with chunks of iron ballast: more than $40,000 in gold was missing.

Captain Foster's relatives hired Daniel Webster, the famous lawyer who argued with the Devil, to sue the bank. They lost the case, as the court did not find the bank liable. But public opinion did hold the bank responsible; people took their money elsewhere and the bank failed. However, despite the question of who was at fault, the greater question was where was the gold and who had taken it? The mystery was never solved and it was a source of curiosity and speculation for many years.

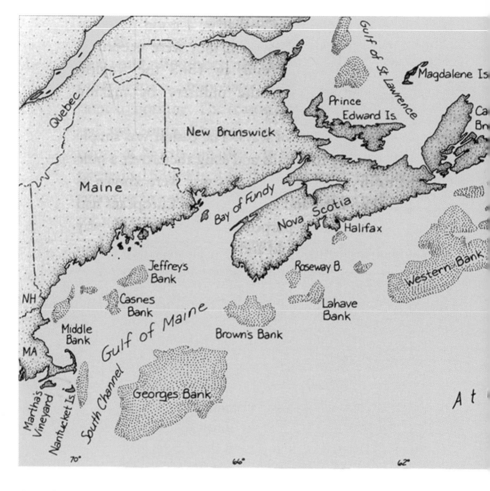

Grand Banks map. *Courtesy of the Marblehead Museum & Historical Society.*

The Grand Banks

Marblehead did recover from the embargos of 1807 and 1812. The fishing fleet grew, and fishing, the processing of salt cod and all the related businesses in the town became prosperous again. Fishing schooners made their way to the Grand Banks on a regular basis. Some crews continued to fish with hand-lines from the decks of their vessels, but increasingly fishing from dories took over as the most efficient way to catch fish. The boats were stored on the decks of the schooners until they reached the Grand Banks. When the ships were

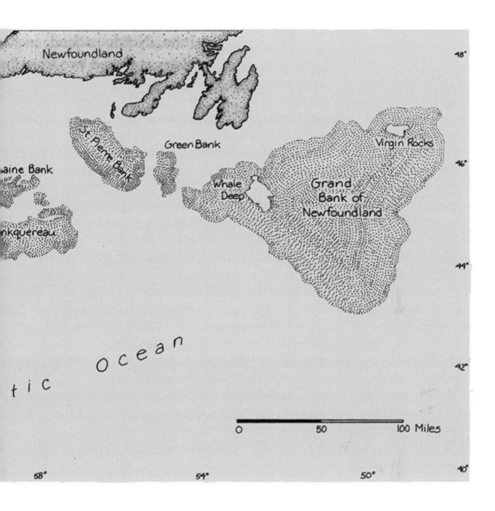

anchored, the dories, each with one or two men, would set off daily to fish for giant cod and halibut.

When looking at a map, the distance between Marblehead and the Grand Banks, located several hundred miles off the coast of Nova Scotia, is enormous. The question that comes to mind immediately is why anyone would go so far away to fish? Wasn't this just making a difficult job even harder than necessary? Fish were to be had right

The Great Gale of 1846, J.O.J. Frost, house paint on wallboard, circa 1920s. *Courtesy of the Marblehead Museum & Historical Society.*

in Marblehead Harbor and were certainly plentiful in the wide ocean beyond the harbor. The answer is that the Grand Banks are legendary fishing grounds and their lure has been felt for centuries. Vikings and Norsemen came to the Grand Banks to fish, as did the Basques. These were special, secret, almost magical fishing grounds, worth the trip and a jealously guarded secret by those who knew the way.

The Grand Banks are special because they are shallow areas deep in the North Atlantic, formed by mountaintops and ranges that reach hundreds of feet above the ocean floor. They reach high enough to allow sunlight to filter through the ocean and cause vegetation to grow.

Plankton and other nourishment are there in abundance. The Grand Banks are a giant feeding ground, a smorgasbord for all the fish in the North Atlantic. Big fish and little fish all make their way there. They come to feed, to mate and to lay their eggs. Big fish eat little fish and fishermen still come for those big fish. The long trip is well worth the effort, because it is always good fishing at the Grand Banks.

Getting there, however, was not quick or easy. From Marblehead the trip took seven days. Once the fishing schooners reached the Banks it took several weeks, under good conditions, to catch enough fish to fill the hold. Weather conditions on the Grand Banks are treacherous always. The reasons that the Banks make such excellent fishing grounds are the same reasons that make them dangerous. The distance from shore makes them isolated, and the relative shallowness of the ocean makes them susceptible to thick blinding fog that rolls in quickly. The open northern Atlantic is vulnerable to hurricanes and huge storms, often causing heavy seas and tremendous waves as tall as skyscrapers.

When fishing schooners were anchored on the Banks, they were at the mercy of all these things. Dory fishermen were at risk every day as they set off in their small boats. They carried with them food, water, foghorns and noisemakers. If a fog rolled in while they were fishing, it was sometimes so thick and all consuming that it made any hope of finding the way back to the "mothership" impossible. Dory men would use the foghorns and noisemakers to alert the crew aboard their fishing sloop of their location. Then the crew would use their own foghorns to try to guide the dories back. Sometimes it worked and sometimes it didn't.

There were many stories of dory fishermen lost at sea. These men were seen as folk heroes, and have been compared to the cowboys of the American West. They were taciturn, tough and had their own code of honor and love. Stories of the dory men of Gloucester are legendary, and the most famous is the legend of Harry Blackburn, who found himself hopelessly lost in a fogbank, unable to get back to his ship. He courageously froze his hands to the oars of his dory to row to Halifax with the dead body of his young dory mate because he had promised the boy's mother that he would not let the lad lie in a watery grave. Blackburn's tavern in Gloucester, which still exists, was given to him by the townsfolk in gratitude for his heroism. Blackburn, who lost both hands to frostbite, ran the tavern for the rest of his life, as he could never go to sea again. Harry Blackburn's story and his name are remembered in part because he is symbolic of all the fishermen who have lost life and limb and whose names are now forgotten.

The Great Gale of 1846

In September of 1846 there were many fishing vessels on the Grand Banks. They were not just from Marblehead, but from fishing towns all along the coast of New England. On September 19 a storm came up suddenly. By nine o'clock in the morning it could be seen in the distance, and the sky darkened as the day went on. At three o'clock in the afternoon the hurricane reached the Banks with tremendous force and fury. It hit the small fishing vessels hard and fast, snapping masts and tossing the ships over huge waves. Each vessel was at the

The Seaman's Monument, lithograph. Erected in honor of the sixty-five men lost at sea in the Great Gale of 1846. *Illustration from* Nooks and Corners of New England, *S.A. Drake, 1875.*

mercy of the sea. The men on board couldn't help themselves and they couldn't help each other. By midnight it was all over, and with the dawn survivors saw the destruction that was left behind, the remains of many ships and men.

It was a devastating storm. Eleven vessels from Marblehead were lost that day, and 65 men were drowned. When the sad news and the survivors made it back to town, they were met by 43 widows and 155 fatherless children who all mourned together. For a small town like Marblehead, there was no one who was not affected in some way by the tragedy. The storm had another significance as well. It had created such a major blow to the town's fishing industry that it marked the end of fishing as the major occupation of the people of Marblehead. There is a monument on Old Burial Hill, a white obelisk that honors the men lost at sea and also stands as a marker for the loss of a way of life.

The *Flying Cloud*

The *Flying Cloud* was a beautiful clipper ship that became one of the most famous ships of its time. Clipper ships are known for their elegant lines and amazing speed. They were the last great sailing ships, built at the end of the Age of Sail.

When gold was discovered in California in 1848, the focus for many in the United States suddenly went from East to West. There was a frenzy to get to the gold fields as quickly as possible. This need for speed caused clipper ships to be designed and built. Those first to arrive in California had the best chance to find gold, and there was a huge demand for fast passenger ships to take them there.

The *Flying Cloud* was designed by Donald McKay, a renowned naval architect, and built at the shipyards in East Boston. She was huge, beautiful and built to challenge existing speed records. Her captain was chosen specifically to break the speed records as well. He was Captain Josiah Perkins Creesy of Marblehead, known as "Perk."

Creesy and his wife Eleanor Prentiss Creesy had grown up together in Marblehead. After their marriage Perk and "Nellie" always sailed together and she became his navigator. They made many voyages around the world, and their trips to China and the Far East were noted for efficiency and speed. They were the obvious choice for the *Flying Cloud*.

There was great excitement, fanfare and frenzied betting on the maiden voyage of the *Flying Cloud* from New York to San Francisco. The results were enormously successful and the ship and crew set an unprecedented record that even today remains impressive. The *Flying Cloud* left New York on June 2 and arrived in San Francisco on August 31, 1851. The voyage took 89 days and 21 hours, breaking the previous record of 120 days. It was the fastest ever, until two years later when Perk Creesy broke his own record.

Though the Creesys spent most of their adult lives at sea, they were considered Marbleheaders. There was great pride in the accomplishments of both of them. Nellie was certainly unique as a female navigator, and Perk was admired for his nautical skills and well beloved as a good and fair captain.

At the end of his career, Creesy came out of retirement to captain the *Ino* during the Civil War. His crew was almost all from Marblehead. Creesy proved that he hadn't lost his skill when he set a new record for crossing the Atlantic in twelve days. He was on his way to Cadiz, where he set about his real job of successfully confining Confederate ships to the harbor, thereby preventing them from returning to the South with weapons and supplies.

The Underground Railroad

Slavery was abolished in Massachusetts in 1780, and the importation of slaves into the United States became illegal in 1808. But slavery continued in the South and slave traders smuggled slaves into the United States under foreign flags. William Lloyd Garrison led the public attack on slavery in his newspaper *The Liberator,* and the New England Anti-Slavery Society was formed in 1832. Many chapters were established in towns on the North Shore, including Marblehead. Their focus was to raise consciousness about the evils of slavery and to help runaway slaves. The Underground Railroad already existed, but abolitionist groups provided additional support. The Underground Railroad was formed and supported by free blacks, escaped slaves, Quakers and other sympathetic whites. Slaves on the run needed to be gotten out of the country and Marblehead's port was an ideal location to transfer slaves from land to sea. The small islands around the mouth of Marblehead's harbor were perfect for ships to hide behind, and provided cover for small vessels or dories to carry slaves out to waiting ships. Slaves came to Marblehead by sea from New York and New Bedford. They came by land in wagons or carriages with false bottoms. Sometimes they used the real railroad, which occasionally became a part of the Underground Railroad. Slaves were smuggled onto trains in Boston, and some sympathetic train men were in on the plan. The Underground Railroad had its own code and slaves were referred to as "packages" and those who helped them were called "conductors." As a train neared an overpass it would slow down, and when a "delivery" was to be made it would go even more slowly. A signal from a lantern would indicate that it was safe, and "packages" would jump off the train at the underpass. Runaway slaves were then hidden in wagons and carriages to be smuggled to their next location.

In Marblehead, slaves were often taken to the most well-known house, that of Simeon Dodge. Betsy and Simeon Dodge lived at 236 Washington Street. The house still exists and is privately owned. The Dodges sheltered and helped many runaway slaves, and they arranged for other safe houses in the town. Another abolitionist said of the Dodges, "It was much easier in those days to make speeches than to *do the work* and run the constant risks—which was cheerfully done and bravely borne by the noble Simeon Dodge and his wife of Marblehead." One of the many slaves helped by the Dodges was Henry "Box" Brown. His story is a tribute to the bravery of both escaping slaves and those who helped them. Henry Brown was born into slavery in Virginia. He was married and had three children. His wife and children were sold to another owner and taken to North Carolina. He never saw them again. After that he decided to escape and came up with an ingenious plan. A large wooden box, two feet wide and three feet long, was made and Henry Brown was placed inside it, with one hole for air and some food and supplies. His box was labeled and taken to the train station, where he was shipped from Richmond to antislavery supporters in Philadelphia. Henry "Box" Brown spent twenty-six hours on his journey. When he was let out of the box, the first thing he said to his rescuers was, "How do you do, gentlemen?" His story became famous and so did Henry. He went on to become a well-known speaker for the Anti-Slavery Society.

Slaves were hidden in safe houses throughout Marblehead. Most locations cannot be confirmed. Slaves were hidden in attic rooms or cellar storage spaces. They were put into secret staircases and closets with fake walls. All of these hiding places existed already, used by Marbleheaders to hide smuggled goods long before they hid human contraband. Not all the houses that have secret rooms were on the Underground Railroad, but the town was well supplied with hiding places. In their secret locations, runaway slaves waited, sometimes days, but frequently only hours, for the signal that a vessel was waiting to take them on the next step of their journey. Slaves were put into dories in the dark of night and rowed out to ships usually bound for Halifax, Nova Scotia. Sometimes they were taken to Newburyport or Maine as an intermediate step, but the final destination was Canada, where they would be out of the range of bounty hunters and enraged slave owners, who sometimes tracked their slaves themselves.

As time went on it became more and more dangerous to hide and help runaway slaves. The Fugitive Slave Act of 1850 made it illegal, punishable by a large fine and prison, to help an escaped slave. It also gave law officers the right to track and capture slaves anywhere they found them. Marblehead abolitionists took their covert activities even further underground, but continued to smuggle slaves. They listened to Frederick Douglass of Lynn speak of his own early life as a slave and were even more committed. Increased awareness of the human suffering that slavery inflicted was spread with the publication of *Uncle Tom's Cabin* by Harriet Beecher Stowe. Marbleheaders were also aware of the economic risks of opposing slavery, as it did affect the sale of shoes made in the North, including those made in shoe factories in the town. But Marblehead continued to be an important point of departure on the Underground Railroad.

The escaped slaves who finally arrived in Halifax were welcomed by a large black community. It was often the site of joyous family reunions as husbands, wives, parents and children were reunited. Though information and documentation about the Underground Railroad is hard to come by, as everything was kept secret and little was written down, confirmation of Marblehead's role still exists in Halifax. When escaped slaves arrived in Canada they often had no last name, or if they did it was the family name of their former owners. There were many reasons to abandon those names. When they were asked for a name, many ex-slaves recalled the friends who had helped them to escape and used their names. In the black community that still thrives in Halifax there are many Marblehead family names, a tribute to the bravery of those who escaped from slavery and the courage of those who helped them.

Another Marblehead native had an important role in the long fight for freedom from slavery. Joseph Story was born in Marblehead, and grew up in a house with seventeen brothers and sisters. His father was a well-known Marblehead doctor. His uncle, Dr. Elisha Story, was a member of the Sons of Liberty and one of the "Indians" at the Boston Tea Party. Joseph Story studied law and went on to become the youngest Supreme Court justice at the age of thirty-two. Story was the judge for the trial of the Africans arrested for mutiny on board the ship *Amistad*. These men had been captured in Africa and taken aboard the Spanish schooner to be transported to the Caribbean to be sold as slaves. They mutinied, captured the ship and then were arrested and tried for mutiny. In 1841 the Supreme Court, with Chief Justice Story presiding, heard the case and declared the Africans free men. They determined that the men had acted in self-defense as kidnapping victims. This decision was a significant victory for the abolitionist movement and equal rights in the United States.

Marblehead and the Civil War

On April 15, 1861, in response to the attack on Fort Sumter, President Abraham Lincoln announced that the United States had declared war on the Confederate states. Lincoln put out a call for 75,000 men to join the Union army. Sent by newspaper and telegraph throughout the United States, the message was received in Marblehead the same day. Marblehead in the 1860s was a small town of fishermen and shoemakers whose traditions of patriotism and loyalty were ingrained. The three Marblehead militia companies responded immediately and prepared to take the early morning train to Boston the next day. On April 16 the earliest train was filled with the first two militia from Marblehead, with the third militia following on the next train. All were eager to defend their country.

When the Marblehead militias arrived in Boston they were greeted by an excited crowd, and they marched to Faneuil Hall, their fifes and drums playing "Yankee Doodle." General Hurk's report reads: "The patriotic men of Marblehead were the first to leave home, and the first to arrive in Boston." The honor of being first was felt by the whole town and Marblehead felt it had once again distinguished itself in American history.

The captains of the three militia were heroes before a shot was fired and their names are still remembered today. They were Captain Knott Martin of the Sutton Light Infantry, Captain Richard Phillips of the Lafayette Guards and Captain Francis Boardman of the Glover Light Guards.

A fourth regiment, known as the Mugford Guards, was organized a month later and the whole town rallied to help it get ready. The new soldiers had no uniforms, and the town schoolteachers donated material for them to be made. A local tailor donated his services to cut out the uniforms. Ladies volunteered their time and spent an entire day and night sewing. When all was ready and the militia was prepared, they attended services at St. Michael's Church and each was given a copy of the Book of Common Prayer. In a speech to the departing company, Selectman William Brown said,

> But if the fortunes of war—always dark and uncertain—keep some of you back forever, we will take courage from your example, and stronger than ever stand by the Union which, from the day of its birth until now, has rained blessings on us all. The muster roll of your gallant band is written on all our hearts. Not a man of you will be forgotten, nor shall the loved ones you leave behind be neglected. Every name shall be cherished in the fond hope of return and reunion; and if any comes not back again, we will write them on the virgin leaves of the history we all love and honor, we will recount them to the future as proofs of your supreme devotion to Liberty, and as pledges that the sons of Marblehead will be true to her forever.

The early days of the war were a time of hope and belief that the conflict would be short, and that victory would come quickly. That early enthusiasm and excitement was soon dulled when news reached Marblehead of the death of three of their own in the battle of Roanoke Island, North Carolina. Many men from Marblehead were stationed in North Carolina in the early part of the war. The first to die in battle was John P. Goodwin, in February of 1862. Optimism soon led to the grim reality of a brutal and bloody war. Through the course of the Civil War the town sent 1,048 men to fight; 112 men made the ultimate sacrifice, and scores of men and boys were wounded. The story of Marblehead's part in the Civil War is similar to that of men all over the United States. Some lived, some died and many were wounded. All were subjected to the horrors of war, as were their wives and families.

During the course of the Civil War, more and more men were needed to fight. The call for soldiers was responded to many times by the town of Marblehead, and younger and younger boys went off to fight. The desire to alleviate the suffering of those in the war was felt keenly by everyone on the homefront. Town organizations and women's groups raised money and made sacrifices to help the soldiers. Even schoolchildren worked for the war effort. One task they did was to laboriously scrape pieces of linen cloth to produce lint that would be used as cotton for bandages for wounded soldiers.

Throughout the war, church bells announced news of every Union victory to the town. On April 8, 1865, the news of the surrender of General Lee at Richmond was received and the church bells rang loudly throughout Marblehead, to the relief and joy of all. But less than a week later the news of the assassination of President Lincoln came as a shocking and tragic end to the Civil War. On the day of Lincoln's funeral, homes, factories and public buildings were draped in mourning, and the church bells tolled sadly.

When the war ended veterans returned home to a society forever changed. They banded together to form the Grand Army of the Republic, or the GAR. The organization was patterned along the lines of many fraternal organizations as a men's group of elected members. They met regularly and raised money through dues and donations to help veterans and their families. They wanted to maintain not a hollow victory of Northern superiority over the South, but a continuation of the United States as a whole. Its membership grew large enough to have political impact, and the GAR was responsible for national legislation that provided pensions for soldiers. Until this time all who served in the U.S. armed forces received no benefits. The GAR-sponsored legislation is seen as one of the first large-scale lobbying efforts in American politics.

Marblehead's GAR Post #82 is named after the town's first Civil War casualty, John P. Goodwin. The post was very active, and

The Old Town House and Market Square, lithograph. *Illustration from* Nooks and Corners of New England, *S.A. Drake, 1875.*

eventually its headquarters were located on the top floor of the Old Town House. It is still there today, left to the Marblehead Historical Society by the last Civil War veterans. The Marblehead GAR post is unique in New England, and possibly the entire United States, because its inner meeting room remains exactly as it was during the time of its use. It is frozen in time, the meeting place of many Civil War veterans who came to support each other with friendship, memories and a financial helping hand. Their ghosts are still in the room, silent and invisible. The large Bible, mounted on a flag-draped stand, is said to remain open to the same page that was read on the day of the last meeting. Four ornately carved chairs face each other on all four sides of the room. Flags of the United States and portraits of their heroes, Washington, Lincoln and Ulysses S. Grant, are at the front of the room. The walls are filled with photographs and mementos of their time at war.

The artifacts in this room were accumulated over a long period of time, and each meant something to the person who donated it. On one wall is a framed Confederate flag. It is a trophy of war that reminded veterans of its story. Captain Richard Phillips was marching at the head of his company through the streets of Newbern, North Carolina. A Southern woman leaned over a high fence and waved the flag directly in his face as a show of contempt. Phillips snatched the flag away from her and carried it home. It remains as a symbol of the war and the emotions felt by both Union and Confederate sympathizers. The GAR was formed in part to allow these emotions to be put aside so that the United States could continue to be a strong union. But it was also formed as a place to remember, a place where veterans who knew all the stories could meet and talk and live through those times again. As Abraham Lincoln said, "Fellow citizens, we cannot escape history."

Abbot Hall and *The Spirit of '76*

As the United States approached its one hundredth year, citizens planned all sorts of celebrations, parades, events and memorials. The new nation was bursting with pride at reaching its one-hundred-year anniversary. In Marblehead there were many events planned for the Fourth of July, including the first Antique and Horribles parade of children in costumes. The Horribles parade continues today and prizes are still awarded for all sorts of categories, including best political commentary.

Most lasting of all the things planned for the centennial was the construction of Marblehead's new town hall. The Old Town House, built in 1727, had served the town well, but it had become too small. Marblehead native Benjamin Abbot made a generous bequest to his hometown, donating funds to be used for a town hall. After some debate about the location, Training Field Hill, at the top of a rise on Washington Street, was chosen. The cornerstone was laid in 1876, and within a year an impressive red brick building in American

Gothic Romanesque style was built. It was and is a large and imposing structure.

Abbot Hall has become a symbol of Marblehead, visible from almost everywhere in town, and a prominent feature of the townscape that rises above the harbor. There are stained-glass windows, large meeting and office rooms and an auditorium on the second floor. The building has an impressive bell tower, with its clock visible in a white diamond pattern. The bell tower is topped by a weathervane. Of special importance within the building is the selectmen's room. Marblehead has been governed by selectmen since the 1600s, and they meet weekly in this room. The room is also a showplace for other Marblehead treasures, including a painting that is a great source of pride for the town, *The Spirit of '76*.

The story of *The Spirit of '76* and its eventual resting place in Marblehead is this. In 1876 there were many paintings made that related to the attitude, character and qualities demonstrated by the Founding Fathers as they planned a new form of government, wrote the Declaration of Independence and fought for freedom. These images were planned for exhibit at the Centennial Exposition in Philadelphia, and for traveling exhibits around the nation.

One of the most popular paintings on display was by Archibald Willard. Willard was a self-trained artist living in Cleveland, Ohio. He made his living painting shop signs and decorations on wagons. He began *The Spirit of '76* as a humorous drawing that he planned to have printed as a color lithograph, and he called it *Yankee Doodle*. In fact, he always referred to the painting by that name. He posed three figures in his studio. The old man in the center, the drummer, was his father. The fife player was a friend who had actually played the instrument in war time, and the young boy was the grandson of General John Devereux. Devereux was a native of Marblehead who lived in Ohio.

When the painting was first displayed in Philadelphia it created a sensation. Everyone loved it, and President Ulysses S. Grant praised it. The painting traveled to other locations, including the Old South Meeting House in Boston. After its triumphal tour, Willard's masterwork was purchased by General Devereux and given to the town of Marblehead. The general asked that it be placed "in Abbot Hall to the memory of the brave men of Marblehead who have died on land and sea for their country." He felt that Marblehead was the perfect place for the painting. Marblehead's history is closely associated with Revolutionary War events, and its patriotism in defending the United States in every war was well known. He could think of no better

The Spirit of '76, Archibald Willard, oil on canvas, 1876. *Courtesy of the Marblehead Museum & Historical Society.*

place for a painting upholding the spirit of democracy. He chose well, for the painting is truly loved by the people of Marblehead.

The Spirit of '76 is a familiar image, used for decades in American history school textbooks. It may not be the greatest work of art, but its heroic figures convey the spirit and determination that makes democracy possible. *The Spirit* remains popular for another reason. It depicts ordinary people who fought for democracy. Most of the other paintings made in 1876 depicted the gentlemanly Founding Fathers, in dress coats and powdered wigs, signing the Declaration of Independence and making speeches. *The Spirit of '76* shows the spirit of the common man, and the heart of democracy.

President Arthur's Visit to Marblehead

In 1882 the president of the United States, Chester A. Arthur, made a visit to Salem as part of a tour of the New England states. He came by government despatch boat and was landed at Dixey's wharf on Marblehead's West Shore. From there he was met by a carriage to take him to Salem.

As he was getting into the carriage a "sad-faced" man came forward and asked the president if he would come and visit the town of Marblehead and speak to the people. President Arthur said that he couldn't, as his schedule was too full. He proceeded to Salem, made his speech there and returned to Marblehead to take the waiting despatch boat.

When his carriage stopped at the wharf, the same man came forward and repeated his request for President Arthur to come into town and meet the people of Marblehead. When the president again said no, the "sad-faced" man jumped into the driver's seat of President Arthur's carriage and drove as fast as he could to Abbott Hall. Church bells, fire alarms and the bell at Abbot Hall all rang furiously as Arthur was driven through the streets. He was met at the town hall by an excited crowd that cheered when he pulled up.

President Arthur was pleased by the response and graciously delivered a short speech. He was then driven back to the West Shore, followed by the exuberant crowd. Arthur cheerfully waved goodbye. He later wrote, "I can never forget the fact that I was once kidnapped in Marblehead." The kidnapper remains unnamed and no charges were ever brought against the "sad-faced" man who delivered such a special treat for the people of Marblehead.

"The Seed King"

James J.H. Gregory made his fortune by accident. He was working as a schoolteacher when he read a notice requesting a good squash seed in the *New England Farmer* magazine. He sent along some seeds that his father had given him. His father had received the seeds from "Marm Hubbard." The squash that grew from them were perfect for the New England climate, hardy, not susceptible to frost and easily grown in rocky soil. Mother Hubbard squash became very popular and from this beginning Gregory built a huge seed business.

Innovative in business, Gregory was an early proponent of seed catalogues. It is said that he was also the inventor of seed envelopes, being the first to design paper packets with pictures and directions for his seeds. He experimented with seeds and plant varieties constantly. Gregory moved an old fish shed from Gerry's Island over to Elm Street to be used as his seed drying headquarters. Known as the "Squash House," it still stands today. Gregory eventually had many fields and farms where he grew a wide variety of plants and flowers for seed.

Gregory also became a great benefactor to Marblehead. When the town built the new town hall, Abbot Hall, in 1876 with proceeds from a bequest from Benjamin Abbot, J.J.H. Gregory donated the bells and clock for the tower. He gave generously of his time and money in support of Marblehead.

Gregory also had a secret. His philanthropy extended beyond the confines of Marblehead. He sent many boxes of books, with bookplates identifying them as from the Marblehead Library, to schools and colleges for Negro students all over the Southern United States. He did this during the last years of his life and never told anyone. His secret was only discovered in the 1960s when a researcher decided to trace the origin of book collections with these bookplates. J.J.H. Gregory was a benevolent man who supported his town, raised eight adopted children and benefited many thousands more with his gift of books.

Chapter 6.

Yachts, Artists and Modern Times

Artists and Yachtsmen Discover Marblehead

Change was felt everywhere after the Civil War. Throughout the rest of the nineteenth and early twentieth centuries everything about the old life changed. In Marblehead the economy shifted. Fishing continued, though not everyone was a fisherman anymore. Shoe factories provided an alternative occupation, and with it a different form of life.

The Industrial Revolution, of which the shoe factories were a part, created workers who were different from the farmers and fishermen who had created the United States. The men and women who worked in factories had something that hadn't really existed before. They had pay packets, received weekly, that gave them cash to pay for their needs. They also had a day off once a week. This combination of time and money made an enormous difference in the way people lived. Interest in and desire for recreation suddenly became an economic force. Factory workers enjoyed amusement parks and trolley car rides.

Factory owners, investors and industrialists were also part of a change in the way people lived. They made enormous sums of money, were unencumbered by income tax and spent lavishly. They emulated

European aristocracy and built American castles, collected fine art and looked for suitable recreation.

Yachting was one form of fashionable recreation. Marblehead, with its deep safe harbor, only seventeen miles from Boston, was an ideal location. In the 1880s the Eastern Yacht Club was established in Marblehead, and its early success in the America's Cup races solidified Marblehead as the "yachting capital of the world." The Corinthian Yacht Club was founded soon after and the Boston Yacht Club established its location in 1902. Yachting races became, and remain, a fixture of the summer season. "Race Week" is still a high point of every summer, when yachts from every class are included and sailors come from around the world to compete.

The end of the nineteenth century saw changes happening fast. The train to Salem added a branch line to Marblehead, and summer visitors began to appear. Hotels and restaurants sprang up to accommodate them. Marblehead Neck, which had been a barren island area connected only to the mainland by a sandbar, was suddenly the site of elegant "summer cottages" built by wealthy yachtsmen. Ferries began shuttling visitors across the harbor from the town to the hotels and yacht clubs on the Neck.

Marblehead's quaint charm, which delighted tourists, was the result of a century of deprivation. Marblehead has so many houses from the eighteenth century because the end of that century and most of the nineteenth century were so economically difficult that no one could afford to update or improve what they had. They were grateful just to have a roof over their heads.

Preservation was not a concern until the twentieth century, when people suddenly realized the architectural treasures that remained. Marblehead has over two hundred homes from the colonial period, clustered in what is now called the Historic District. Set beside the harbor, these houses are crowded together on narrow, winding streets, with tiny gardens and small patches of green space. Marblehead is a gift from the past, but it is not a past that is without cost. Marblehead is what it is today because of its own unique history and the spirit and determination of its citizens.

Marblehead Pottery

Marblehead holds a unique and fascinating place in the history of the American arts and crafts movement. Marblehead Pottery was begun in 1904 as a part of therapy used by Dr. Herbert Hall, a physician trained at Harvard Medical School at a time when there was great interest in social reform. There were many theories that dealt with the treatment of physical and mental ailments with therapy involving handicrafts.

Dr. Hall was a pioneer in the use of occupational therapy for patients suffering from nervous distress. He established a sanitarium in Marblehead. His first patients stayed in boardinghouses, and then he took over the beautiful Devereux Mansion near Devereux Beach. Here he put his theories into practice. He met and collaborated with Jessie Luther, a young woman who had studied at the Rhode Island School of Design and also believed in the power of crafts as therapy. Dr. Hall established his first handicraft shop on Front Street, just off Goodwin's Court. The crafts offered to patients included weaving, pottery and wood and metal work. Soon Dr. Hall hired a young student from Alfred University in New York State to help with the pottery and glazes. Arthur Baggs was a student of Charles Binns, who has been called the father of the arts and crafts movement. Baggs came in the summers and wrote constantly to his teacher, asking for advice and help to perfect his glazes.

Not long after Baggs arrived, Jesse Luther was hired away by Sir Wilfred Grenfell. They went on to establish the still flourishing Grenfell Mission in Newfoundland. The mission works to alleviate the extreme poverty of local fishermen and their families. Jesse Luther founded the hooked rug industry that is still an enormously successful part of Grenfell Handicrafts, which continues to support the work of the mission.

Arthur Baggs created the smooth matte glazes that are distinctive to Marblehead Pottery. As the 1919 catalogue states, it is "a pottery which in its soft colors and tones reflects something of the gay little gardens and old gray streets, something of the rocks and sea." The colors are Marblehead blue, gray, green, wisteria, rose, yellow and tobacco brown. Baggs also developed the Marblehead Pottery forms, which are simple elegant shapes, mostly thrown on a potter's wheel. Many of the pieces are undecorated. The decorated ones use natural motifs, again drawing inspiration from Marblehead with natural forms of local flowers and birds. The decorations are subtle, with designs scored into the clay using colors only slightly different than the color of the piece.

Most of the handicrafts that Dr. Hall offered to his patients as a part of their treatment were successful. But ironically, it soon became

Marblehead Pottery vase with flying geese motif as decorative border, circa 1920s. *Courtesy of the Marblehead Museum & Historical Society.*

clear that the exacting nature of pottery thrown on the wheel was too stressful for most patients. After all, they were not artists or craftspeople when they came to the sanitarium. They usually stayed only for a few weeks or months, and they couldn't learn the craft so quickly. It also became apparent that the colors and shapes that Baggs had designed had great appeal. So Marblehead Pottery became a commercial venture, and for a time the sale of its goods supported Dr. Hall's hospital.

The Marblehead Pottery was sold to Arthur Baggs in 1915. The business made and sold its wares at 11 Front Street, and had a successful mail-order operation as well, using a small catalogue that described the pottery and its aesthetic philosophy. When King Tut's tomb was opened in 1923 it was a sensation, and there was enormous interest in all things Egyptian. Marblehead Pottery received an order for one thousand perfume bottles to be modeled after one taken from the tomb. The actual perfume container was sent to Marblehead and a mold was made. It bears the Marblehead Pottery stamp, and was made in several shades of blue and green. These perfume bottles were sold in New York and were very popular. Marblehead Pottery was one of several art pottery lines carried by Tiffany's and several other exclusive shops in the 1920s.

Marblehead Pottery was produced from 1904 to 1936, and the studio finally closed its doors in 1940. A wide variety of artists worked at the studio over the years, including John Selmer Larson and Arthur Wesley Dow. Sometimes the pottery operated year round and sometimes just for the summer months. Arthur Baggs eventually went to Ohio State University to head its ceramics department and only came to Marblehead in the summer. There were few records kept, much to the frustration of Marblehead Pottery collectors. It is almost impossible to date much of the pottery, as many of the styles were made for the entire thirty years. Marblehead Pottery has a distinctive makers' mark. In the center is a square-rigged sailing ship, flanked by an M and P. After 1915 the pottery also had a paper label. However, this is not consistent, as the stamps were sometimes misplaced or forgotten and many experimental designs, shapes and colors were not stamped or marked at all. Individual designers sometimes scored their pieces with their initials, but this has also led to confusion. HT is frequently attributed to Hannah Tutt, who was the bookkeeper for the pottery and probably did not make any pots herself. Other artists came and went, as artists do, and many of their names are not known.

Marblehead Pottery continues to become increasingly famous. It is collected by celebrities and millionaires. Stories abound of the fabulous sums received for pieces that originally sold for a dollar or two. Some Marbleheaders still remember buying a small bud vase for fifty cents. For the most part, the fabulous sums are for large decorated pieces. As with all ceramics, the value is severely affected by damage. But Marblehead Pottery continues to have a mystique and an important place in the art of the twentieth century.

Flying High

W. Starling Burgess was a pioneer of early aviation. He was a daredevil and a genius who is best remembered as a yacht designer. But for a brief time in his long career he was captivated by aeroplanes. He met the Wright brothers in 1908 and soon began designing planes. He set up a workshop in Marblehead on Redstone Lane, facing Marblehead Harbor, where he began building wooden planes. His first success was on February 28, 1910, when he transported his newly constructed plane, called the *Flying Fish*, to Chebacco Lake in Hamilton. Burgess and his partner Augustus Herring invited reporters from major New York and Boston newspapers to record the event. They wanted publicity and Burgess promised plenty of drinks and cigars even if the flight wasn't a success. The frozen lake served as the runway from which the *Flying Fish* took off and made aviation history. It was the first flight in New England. The plane did not go very far or very fast, but it flew on its own and that was enough.

The next year, 1911, was a succession of firsts. Burgess was the first civilian student of the Wright Brothers Flying School. Interestingly enough he learned to fly after he had built several airplanes and flown them. Burgess began the first airplane factory in New England. One of the pilots for Burgess Company set several flying records. Harry Atwood, of Swampscott, seemed to have an aptitude both for flying and for getting publicity. Less than a year after the *Flying Fish*'s half-mile flight, Atwood flew a Burgess plane all the way to New York City, where he dramatically circled the Statue of Liberty before landing. After that he was news, so his flight to Washington, D.C., was followed by newspapers all over the country. Atwood needed another newsworthy landing, so he brought his plane down on the White House lawn. President Taft came out to greet the "King of the Air." Atwood's most famous flight was from St. Louis to New York City in a record-setting twelve days. In 1911 Burgess also began experimenting with a hydroplane that could take off and land on water.

In 1912 history was made again when Marblehead became the official birthplace of marine aviation. Lieutenant Anstel Cunningham of the U.S. Marine Corps flew a Burgess plane out of Marblehead Harbor. The plane was a prototype of the Burgess-Dunne that became the most successful of the Burgess planes. It was sold to Canada as a warplane before the United States entered World War I. The Burgess-Dunne was also sold to civilians, including millionaire playboy Vincent Astor, who came to Marblehead in his yacht and towed his new plane home in its specially designed floating hangar.

The Burgess factory expanded to Little Harbor, and at its wartime peak it produced more than one thousand planes and employed eight hundred people. To this day, Burgess Co. is the largest employer the town has ever known. After the United States entered World War I, Burgess joined the U.S. Navy and began flying planes as well as building them. The Burgess factory burned down on the night of the "false Armistice," an incorrect report that occurred just days before the real armistice on November 11, 1918.

After the end of the war and the fire, the Burgess airplane factory closed. There was a lull in airplane production after the war ended and before commercial aviation began that resulted in no new orders for airplanes. Burgess went back to yacht design and had great success. He designed several America's Cup winners and defenders. He also continued to be attracted to new forms of transportation, and he designed and built a small submarine and he and Buckminster Fuller experimented with a three-wheeled car.

There are many stories about Starling Burgess and his aeroplane antics during the time he was in Marblehead. The planes were all biplanes, and there is a story of a daring young woman from Marblehead Neck who sat on one of the wings as Burgess flew over the harbor. There is also a story that Burgess dressed a stuffed teddy bear in children's clothes and threw it from his plane, to the horror of onlookers. Certainly Burgess lived a life that was full of excitement, adventure, triumph and tragedy. He was married five times and his first wife committed suicide. His son drowned in Marblehead Harbor. His daughter, also named Starling Burgess, changed her name and became the well-known children's book illustrator Tasha Tudor. Starling Burgess didn't live in Marblehead for long, but he made his mark in the world of aviation as well as on the history and legends of Marblehead.

W. Starling Burgess on the wing of one of his planes, built for the U.S. Navy, circa 1912.
Courtesy of the Marblehead Museum & Historical Society.

J.O.J. Frost: Grandma Moses of Marblehead

John Orne Johnson Frost was born in Marblehead in 1852. He grew up on Front Street, in a house near the harbor and the public landing. In Frost's boyhood the landing was the center of activity for fishermen, both active and retired. Children gravitated there as well, and as they played and fished, they listened to endless stories. The men talked about fishing on the Grand Banks and told tales of Marblehead's glorious days in the American Revolution and of sea battles in the War of 1812. All the stories were filled with the sense of pride that the old-timers felt about the town.

J.O.J. Frost went to sea at the age of sixteen, making his first voyage on the fishing schooner *Josephine*, bound for the Grand Banks. All went well and he signed on for a second trip, this time aboard the *Oceana*. On their return trip, in April of 1869, the vessel was suddenly engulfed in a freak snowstorm. Visibility was at zero. With freezing conditions, the crew took turns in fifteen-minute shifts to man the tiller. Like all the schooners at that time, the ship was entirely wind powered and had no instruments except a compass and sextant. They knew they were off course, but with not even a horizon line to orient them there was no way to get their bearings, and all hands feared the worst. They thought they were doomed. Then, just as suddenly as it had started, the storm disappeared and the *Oceana* was able to find her way back to Marblehead.

When Frost reached home he never went to sea again. He married his sweetheart, Annie Lillibridge, and they both went to work in her father's restaurant. He eventually owned a restaurant of his own and also ran a bakery. Frost held a variety of jobs in his lifetime, working as a cook, a carpenter and occasionally writing for the local newspaper.

Eventually Frost joined his wife Annie in her business. Annie had planted a few fields with flowers beside their home on Pond Street. This was considered unusual at the time, when most land was used for edible crops. One day a summer resident from the Neck came by and saw a few flower bouquets that Annie sometimes put out by the road to sell. The lady was delighted and asked for as many as her carriage would hold to decorate tables for a luncheon party she was giving the next day. Annie obliged. When the woman asked the price, Annie said she could have them at no cost. The woman refused, and said she could give Annie a lot of business if she was interested. She knew that the other ladies on the Neck would follow her lead. In fact, she was right and Annie Frost's sweet peas became all the rage. Her business became so successful that she was featured in a 1918 edition of *McCall's* ladies magazine as an entrepreneur. Frost helped sell her flowers from a wheelbarrow that he trundled down to Market Square on summer days.

It was after Annie's death that Frost began his final career. Frost deeply missed his wife and was lonely. He had all sorts of stories to tell and no one to listen to him. He also had a deep love for Marblehead, and wanted to ensure that its history was remembered. Why he chose painting as his medium is unknown. He could have written stories, songs or poems about the town. But, like Grandma Moses, Frost chose painting as his medium.

In 1922, at the age of seventy, J.O.J. Frost began to paint. As he himself said, "Never painted a picture until I was past seventy years young." Frost had never been trained as an artist. He used materials he had on hand—house paint, wall board and odds and ends of wood scraps—to create his works. He had no understanding of perspective, no knowledge of anatomy and no particular skill at drawing. When images failed him he often wrote misspelled descriptions, mostly in white paint, at odd angles all over the paintings. What might be considered artistic failings in fact make his paintings charming and unique.

Frost did have talent, in his ability to compose a scene and record events. Much of his subject matter was scenes from Marblehead history, starting with the founding of the town and working his way through to the proud moments of the Civil War. He considered himself a historian rather than an artist.

Frost also created scenes of fishing on the Grand Banks. When he made these paintings it had been more than fifty years since he had been to sea. But his memories remained strong. He painted the vessel *Oceana* lost in the snowstorm. He painted a true account of a man thrown overboard, and of ropes thrown out in a vain attempt to try to rescue him. He painted seabirds and fish and whales, including whales at play. He remembered everything from those two voyages and the endless stories he had heard from the fisherman at the town landing.

He also painted many pictures of the town of Marblehead as he remembered it from his boyhood. By the time Frost started painting in 1922, the town of his boyhood was not just disappearing; it was gone. The small fishing town that Frost's paintings record is the Marblehead of post–Civil War 1860s and '70s: the harbor filled with fishing schooners, chickens, cows and pigs in most of the yards, and every house with a kitchen garden of vegetables. Oxen pulled heavy loads of wood and iron anchors, and horse and buggies or stagecoaches were the transportation available. By 1922 Marblehead Harbor was filled with pleasure yachts and restaurants. Grocery stores were abundant, and cars and trucks had taken over the roads.

Frost worked tirelessly on his paintings, carvings and ship models. He often put his work in an open wheelbarrow and walked down to Market Square, trying to sell the paintings for twenty-five or fifty cents. He didn't have much luck. He was friendly with the local photographer, Fred Litchman, who owned a photo studio on Washington Street. He would bring a newly completed work down to Litchman's and Fred would make a picture of the new painting, usually including Frost in the photo. He also allowed Frost to display his latest work in his shop window. Many people came to see Frost's latest effort, but not to admire it. They laughed and made fun of his work, scornful that it didn't look like "real" art. This seemed to have almost no effect on Frost, as he went on painting anyway.

Frost eventually built a small building beside his house at 11 Pond Street, which he called his museum. It was covered with his paintings, inside and out, as well as a collection of his carvings and a variety of odd bits of things he had collected over the years, including a piece of wood from "Old Ironsides," ropes and anchors attributed to other ships and his beloved Musical Rocks. It cost twenty-five cents to go to the museum, and the proceeds were donated to the Marblehead Female Humane Society. The Female Humane Society still exists, but it wasn't sustained by large donations from Frost's museum. He had few visitors. Almost everyone who came to his museum was from "away." Frost was discovered by a newspaperman at the *Salem Evening News* who wrote articles about him and his paintings. A few of his paintings sold as a result.

The hardest sell of all was the Musical Rocks. These were and remain a mystery. Frost was crazy about them. He claimed to have been given the rocks by some Indians. The rocks were stacked in formation, and apparently each had a different tone when struck. Frost loved to play the musical rocks for visitors to his museum. He was often quite put out when they couldn't recognize the tunes he played. Whether he was bad at the rocks or they weren't as musical as he thought may never be known. At Frost's death the musical rocks were arranged around his tombstone at Waterside cemetery, but they have since disappeared.

J.O.J. Frost produced over two hundred paintings and carvings before his death in 1928. He left the bulk of his collection to the Marblehead

J.O.J. Frost, circa 1920s. The artist is holding his carved and painted cod. *Courtesy of the Marblehead Museum & Historical Society.*

Historical Society. The paintings were largely ignored for a long time, but after the Second World War there was a surge of national pride. American folk art became popular, sought after and valuable. Frost's paintings are now recognized as fabulous, and there are still a few people left in Marblehead who remember that they could have had one for fifty cents. When Frost's home on Pond Street was sold, and several walls of Frost's paintings were found during remodeling, it took a court case to determine that the paintings were part of the house, and therefore the property of the new owners.

J.O.J. Frost would be proud and happy to know how much his work is admired today. His paintings and carvings have their own permanent exhibit gallery at the Marblehead Museum & Historical Society, and are seen and loved by adults and children from around the world.

Marblehead Arts and the King Hooper Mansion

By the end of the 1920s Marblehead had become an active art community, and had attracted several well-known artists who settled in and developed a strong affection for the town. One of them was Samuel Chamberlain, who led the cause for the Marblehead Arts Association to purchase the 1745 King Hooper Mansion as a permanent home for the organization.

This was accomplished in 1937. Chamberlain and Arthur Heintzelman, another distinguished printmaker who went on to become the first keeper of prints at the Boston Public Library, organized a fund drive to restore the mansion. They formed the Friends of Contemporary Prints, which produced a print subscription series. One print was produced annually from 1939 through the early 1950s. Each was a limited edition of three hundred signed and numbered prints. The artists were all friends of Chamberlain and Heintzelman, and their work forms a solid collection of New England printmakers of the first half of the twentieth century.

The most popular prints in the series are those by Sam Chamberlain. There are several reasons for that. Chamberlain was a superb craftsman and his etchings are beautiful examples of the richness of the medium. Also his prints were Marblehead scenes, and he lived in town. Chamberlain was an enthusiastic and popular resident. He and his wife Narcissa, known as Biscuit, arrived in the 1930s after many years in France. They brought with them their French cook. Chamberlain later wrote a delightful book about her reactions to American life called

Clementine in the Kitchen. Chamberlain lived and worked in Marblehead for the rest of his life, adapting from printmaking to photography. He is better known for his photographic work, mostly of historic houses up and down the East Coast.

One of the other, and certainly the most famous, of the printmakers was Frank W. Benson. In a sense Benson had two careers. He is well known as an American Impressionist for his beautiful images of summer sunlight on healthy, handsome young people. He was equally known for strong technically skilled etchings. By the late 1930s he was the grand old man of etching. He contributed to the series a characteristic print called *Six Bluebills* of ducks in flight. Benson's legacy in Marblehead is carried on by his niece, Beverly Benson Seamans. She is a sculptor, and her work continues Benson's fascination with sea birds. Her bronzes of birds, animals and children are well known in Marblehead and beyond.

Chamberlain, Benson and Seamans are only a few examples of the many artists who have been and continue to be associated with Marblehead and whose work has enriched the quality of life here. A familiar scene throughout the town is artists at work, sketching and painting. Cars and pedestrians are accustomed to keeping a watch out for easels placed for artistic advantage that might cause a traffic hazard.

Isabella Stewart Gardner's Secret Hideaway

There is a small villa on Marblehead Neck built in a Mediterranean style. It is called Twelve Lanterns and was planned, commissioned and supervised during construction by Isabella Stewart Gardner. In its own small way the house is as unique and distinctive as Mrs. Gardner's palace and museum in Boston, known as Fenway Court. In both places Mrs. Gardner used architecture that certainly doesn't evoke New England. She used the decorative tiles, balconies and arched doorways that she saw in her beloved Venice. Twelve Lanterns sits high on rock ledge looking out toward the open Atlantic Ocean. A covered arch and stone steps lead to the entrance of the house. Inside it is not terribly large, though the main room has an enormous fireplace and a raised area designed for a grand piano. In this room is the first of the twelve lanterns that give the house its name. One of the most intriguing features of the house is a square tower accessible only by a sort of hidden trap door. The tower room has twelve large

Marblehead, Samuel Chamberlain, etching, circa 1940s. *Courtesy of Arnould Gallery, Marblehead.*

windows with a limitless view in all directions, taking in the ocean, the harbor and the town.

The house was built in 1910 by Mrs. Gardner, who by that point in her life was a widow. Isabella Stewart Gardner was a well-known patron of the arts. She was also a benefactor to many young artists, in particular to handsome young men who showed promise. Whether Isabella Stewart Gardner had romantic relationships with these young men will probably never be known. But she did support and encourage them. For George Proctor, a talented young pianist who became her protégé, Mrs. Gardner built Twelve Lanterns. She introduced Proctor to influential musicians, sent him to Europe for study and fostered his talent. He was a somewhat difficult protégé, and he did not always apply himself to his music.

Neither Mrs. Gardner nor George Proctor ever lived in the house. Mrs. Gardner gave the house to him as a wedding gift, but he and his wife never moved in. The beautifully designed space for his piano never became the music salon that Mrs. Gardner had planned, and the house was eventually sold.

Eugene O'Neill's Underpants

Out near the lighthouse on Marblehead Neck is a house where Eugene O'Neill and his third wife Carlotta lived in 1948. O'Neill is considered one of the most important American playwrights of the twentieth century. His plays are deeply provoking and memorable, even if they do not always make for the most enjoyable evening at the theater.

By the time O'Neill came to stay on Marblehead Neck he was suffering from Parkinson's disease and was no longer writing. But he was proud of his home and bragged in a letter to Charlie Chaplin that he had turned a "dinky summer cottage" into a beautiful little house for a mere $85,000. O'Neill's life in Marblehead was like one of his plays. He watched the ocean through his binoculars, brooded and had few visitors. Finally it is said that he ran wildly out of the house one night, fell on the ice and broke his leg. He and his wife both were taken to the hospital and they never came back to Marblehead.

Many years later at a charity auction in Marblehead, a pair of men's boxer shorts came up for offer. Tastefully framed, they were reported to be Eugene O'Neill's underpants, salvaged after he left town by a souvenir-seeking parlor maid and handed down in the family. And just possibly that's what they were.

Peaches Point and the Islands

On the other side of Marblehead Harbor is an area called Peaches Point. It was largely uninhabited for over two centuries, with the exception of the Peach family, who settled there in the 1600s and used the area primarily as farm and grazing land. At the end of the nineteenth century that changed when Francis Crowninshield of the Salem shipping family purchased a major portion of the land. He built a large summer home there and soon, like Marblehead Neck, the area became a summer colony. The Crowninshields and particularly Louise DuPont Crowninshield became the "first family" of Peaches Point.

Louise DuPont Crowninshield brought to Marblehead an interest in historic preservation, antiques and a great appreciation for the Jeremiah Lee Mansion. She had grown up at Winterthur and was the sister of Henry DuPont, who established the Winterthur Museum. Mrs. Crowninshield's knowledge of early American furniture and decorative arts was impressive. She was enormously wealthy and rather large. She favored flowered dresses, a mink coat and many, many rings. She was extremely kind, generous and well liked. She knew what she wanted and she usually got it, but she did it nicely and hardly anyone had an unkind word to say about her. Mrs. Crowninshield and her husband owned several homes and followed the fashionable "seasons" as they moved from place to place. Her home at Peaches Point was beautiful, with elegant furnishings and beautiful formal gardens. It was torn down at her death because she didn't want anyone else to live in it.

Just off Peaches Point are three small islands that are just outside the mouth of the harbor. These islands have always been mostly uninhabited or used as summer retreats.

Cat Island was the site a very early smallpox hospital established in colonial times. The idea of inoculating against smallpox using active pox was practiced here. It was a very controversial practice, and finally the hospital was closed down because of negative sentiments. The island was also used as a quarantine area for ships to be inspected before entering the harbor and as a tuberculosis hospital. All in all Cat Island didn't have a very cheerful history until the twentieth century, when it was purchased by the Marblehead/ Swampscott YMCA to be used as a children's summer day camp and its name was changed to Children's Island.

Brown's Island is accessible from the mainland on foot during low tide. Not everyone knows about the tides, and visitors are occasionally

Little Harbor, Charles A. Walker, etching, 1886. *Courtesy of the Marblehead Museum & Historical Society.*

stranded on the island because they don't notice the tide coming in. The island was originally owned by the Wizard Edward Dimond of Orne's Hill fame. What he used it for is anybody's guess. Eventually the island was bought by the Crowninshield family, renamed Crowninshield Island, a name that is almost totally ignored, and given to the Trustees of Reservations. It is maintained as a park and is open to all.

Gerry's Island was the home of one of Marblehead's early parsons, and has sometimes been used for summer residences. It was originally used mainly as pasture land, and cows and goats were led over to the island at low tide. It is privately owned and not open to the public.

The Rindge Family Mystery

On Peaches Point there is a house that has a mysterious past. The Rindge house was built in 1880. It was a beautiful mansion in a perfect location. The Rindge family used it as a summer retreat and moved there each June with their children and servants and always had a wonderful time.

Eventually the family moved to California. But on the day they left, nothing was packed up or put away. When they left the house was completely furnished, to all appearances as if its owners would be back later that day. Everything was left exactly as it had been the day before. And no one ever came, as they usually did in the fall, to close up the house for the winter. Nothing was moved or covered up.

The house stood empty year after year with no explanation as to what had happened. Children in the neighborhood began to sneak into the house to play occasionally. But no one has ever discovered why the house was just left like that. The Rindge family had not fallen on hard times. They moved to Los Angeles and bought large tracts of land and a beautiful seaside estate. But they never came back to Marblehead, never occupied the house again and the house was eventually seized for nonpayment of taxes in 1940. There must be some explanation. It isn't possible that this prosperous family just forgot they had a house in Marblehead, and they couldn't have forgotten to tell someone to take care of it. But the Rindge family mystery remains unsolved.

The USS *Marblehead*

A vessel named the USS *Marblehead* achieved legendary status during World War II. The cruiser was a part of the Battle of the Java Sea in February 1942. It was a fierce fight and the American fleet was hit hard. The *Marblehead* was attacked by twenty-seven Japanese planes, bombed from all directions and reported sunk by the enemy.

Somehow, miraculously she stayed afloat. Despite a shattered steering gear and large gaping holes in her sides, the USS *Marblehead* traveled over thirteen thousand miles to make it back to the United States. It is no wonder that she was called "the ship that wouldn't die." Her exploits became well known when President Franklin D. Roosevelt mentioned the USS *Marblehead* in one of his radio broadcast Fireside Chats, using them as an example of American bravery and determination. The flag and the bell from the vessel are displayed in the selectman's room at Abbot Hall as another example of Marblehead's valor in time of war.

The Beryl Atherton Murder

The murder of Beryl Atherton has become one of the most intriguing mysteries in Marblehead. It continues to be a topic of debate and speculation more than fifty years after the event.

Beryl Atherton was a schoolteacher in Marblehead. She taught fifth grade at the Glover School. By all accounts she was well liked, and many of her former students remember her fondly. Miss Atherton lived alone at 57 Sewell Street. At the end of November in 1950 she was preparing for the coming winter season. On Friday, November 24, she went to Boston to take her fur coat out of storage. On returning to Marblehead she stopped at the local market to buy a few things. Then she went home. It had already started snowing. A nor'easter was producing heavy, wet snow that would eventually bring down electrical wires and immobilize the town for the whole weekend.

When Miss Atherton got home she put her purchases on the kitchen table. She took her trash out and was seen by a boy who was probably the last person to see her alive. She then went upstairs to take off her wet things. She came downstairs in just her slip, leaving her skirt on the upstairs railing to dry. She proceeded to chop up the meat she had bought to feed her little dog. At some point that evening, after the dog was fed but before she had finished dressing, someone came into Beryl Atherton's house and murdered her. The murderer was probably someone she knew.

It was not until the following Monday that the terrible deed was discovered. That morning, the milkman was making his rounds. Miss Atherton's delivery man was known as "Pint" Phillips. He came in the back door as usual, preparing to put the milk in the refrigerator. There he found a grisly scene. Beryl Atherton was lying on her kitchen floor in a pool of blood. Terrified, Pint ran out and got a neighbor. Together they went back, and there was no question as to whether the woman was dead. They called the police.

When they arrived, the policemen were also horrified at the scene. There have been seventeen murders in the 350 years since Marblehead was founded, and none in the experience of the officers involved. Nevertheless they set about recording the evidence and trying to make sense of it. They found pieces of a broken knife in the body. Beside her they found pearls from the broken strand around Miss Atherton's neck. They found blood under the body, but no signs of a struggle. The kitchen had been cleaned up. The little dog was found, alive but frightened in an upstairs closet. There were no fingerprints or footprints to be found, and no sign of a forced entry.

The investigation went on for several months and many townspeople were questioned. The police chief himself admitted that he had probably talked to the murderer, but there was no evidence to charge anyone. There was never an arrest and no murderer was ever named. There was plenty of talk and speculation. Miss Atherton was whispered to have led a double life, although no one knew when or how. There was talk of a rejected lover or a jealous wife, but there was no evidence of either. The police were frustrated by the whole thing. The timing of the storm had given the murderer a chance to go back to the scene of the crime and clean up. No one was ever charged with the crime.

Recently the story has resurfaced due in part to the fascination with cold case crimes. The mystery continues to be intriguing and there are several theorists who claim to know the identity of the murderer. One claims that the murderer is still alive.

Beryl Atherton is certainly not forgotten. Some claim that she is still waiting for the crime to be solved. The Glover School where Miss Atherton taught is an active, lively place in the daytime. Many generations of children have been educated there. It is here that her spirit lingers.

No child has ever seen her, but several teachers have. On the third floor at Glover School, where Miss Atherton's classroom was, teachers have seen an unknown woman in the hallway or in her classroom in the evening. The woman is not menacing and does not try to move toward them. Instead she seems sad and moves slowly around the room before fading away. Could it be the ghost of Beryl Atherton? She loved teaching and her pupils and the Glover School. Does she come back to keep watch over it? Perhaps Miss Atherton is waiting at the school and hoping for her murder to be solved so she can rest in peace.

Delft tile, eighteenth century, detail from fireplace in Jeremiah Lee Mansion. *Courtesy of the Marblehead Museum & Historical Society.*

Conclusion

History is a collection of stories that can be documented. Myths, legends and folklore often cannot be confirmed, and frequently have more than one version. Why bother then to collect or remember them? Is this really a valid way to document our past?

After studying the history of Marblehead, its myths emerge as an important part of the whole. Their truth becomes less important than the sense of the past that they impart. Also significant in their telling is the sense of shared experience and community that they continue to represent.

Popular culture can reveal much about the past. People's hopes and fears remind us of the similarities we share with past generations despite differences made by time and events. The combination of myth, legend and truth set in a chronological framework makes the history of Marblehead come alive.

Marblehead has so many stories. The ones collected here are some of the most famous, or the most favorite. There are many more to tell and many new ones to be made in the future.

Bibliography

Baggs, Arthur. *Marblehead Pottery Catalogue: An American Industrial Art of Distinction*. Marblehead: The Marblehead Potteries, 1919.

Cohn, Amy L. *From Sea to Shining Sea: A Treasury of American Folklore and Folk Songs*. New York: Scholastic, Inc., 1993.

Depauw, Linda Grant. *Seafaring Women*. Boston: Houghton Mifflin, 1982.

Doliber, Donald. "Murder Most Foul: Cold Blooded Murders in Marblehead." Lecture at the Marblehead Museum & Historical Society, October 20, 2004.

Drake, Samuel Adams. *A Book of New New England Legends and Folk Lore*. Boston: Little, Brown and Co., reissued by Singing Tree Press, 1969.

———. *Nooks and Corners of New England*. New York: Harper & Brothers, 1875.

Drake, Samuel Adams, and Samuel Chamberlain. *New England Legends and Folklore*. New York: Hastings House, 1972.

Gamage, Virginia, and Priscilla Lord. *Marblehead: The Spirit of '76 Lives Here*. Philadelphia: Chilton Book Company, 1972.

Goloboy, Joan, and Pam Peterson. *Marblehead in the Civil War.* CD-Rom produced by Marblehead Museum & Historical Society, 2006.

Gotschall, Day, ed. *Marblehead Celebrates 350 Years of Democracy.* Marblehead, 1999.

Gould, Bartlett. "Burgess of Marblehead." *Essex Institute Historical Collections* 106, no. 1 (January 1970).

Grafton, John, ed. *Great Ghost Stories.* Mineola, NY: Dover Publications, Inc., 1992.

Griffen, Ellen M. *Moll Pitcher's Prophecies and the World Renowned Pythoness of Lynn.* Boston: Eastburn Press, 1895.

Hansen, Ellen, ed. *The Underground Railroad: Life on the Road to Freedom.* Perspective on History Series. Carlisle, MA: Discovery Enterprises, Ltd., 1995.

Hercher, Gail Pike. "Marblehead Pottery." *American Art Pottery Monthly,* no. 58 (March 1981).

Jagendorf, M. *New England Beanpot: American Stories to Read and Tell.* New York: Vanguard Press, 1964.

Jones, Bruce, et al. *Abolitionists and the Underground Railroad in the Essex National Heritage Area.* Network to Freedom Initiative of the National Park Service. Salem Maritime National Historic Site, 2003.

Knight, Russell K. *The Headers in Life and Legend.* Marblehead: Legend Publications, 1989.

Lewis and Newhall. *The History of Lynn.* Lynn, MA, 1829.

Miles, Dorothy. *The Wizard of Orne Hill and Other Tales of Marblehead.* Marblehead: self-published, 1985.

Moore, John Hamilton. *The New Practical Navigator: Being an Epitome of Navigation.* London: B. Law and Son, 1793.

Murray, Lieutenant. *Fanny Campbell the Female Pirate Captain: A Tale of the Revolution.* Boston: F. Gleason, 1845.

O'Neill, J.P. *The Great New England Sea Serpent*. Down East Books, 1999.

Peterson, Pam. *J.O.J. Frost Gallery Guide*. Marblehead: MarbleheadMuseum & Historical Society, 2003.
———. *Wish You Were Here: Souvenir Postcards of Marblehead*. Marblehead: Marblehead Museum & Historical Society, 2002.

Provenzano, Richard G. "Pirates Glen & Dungeon Rock: The Evolution of a Legend." Saugus Historical Society, booklet no. 3, 1987.

Roads, Samuel, Jr. *The History and Traditions of Marblehead*. Marblehead: Allen Lindsey & Co., 1897.

Welsch, Ulricke. *Marblehead*. Beverly, MA: Commonwealth Editions, 2000.

Whittier, John Greenleaf. *The Poetry of John Greenleaf Whittier: A Reader's Edition*. IN: Friends United Press, 2000.

Index

About the Author

P am Peterson is the director of the Marblehead Museum & Historical Society. Originally trained as a fine arts conservator, she has worked at the Isabella Stewart Gardner Museum, the University of Heidelberg manuscript department, the Fogg Museum and the Peabody Essex Museum. She lives in Marblehead with her husband and two children.

Visit us at
www.historypress.net